Praise for
Free Byrd: The Power of a Liberated Life

"I have been in a Bible study with Paul Byrd for almost a decade. When he raises his hand to speak I get excited because I know it's going to be good. After reading *Free Byrd*, I now feel the same way about his writing. Get ready!"

—Jeff Foxworthy

"Ask any major league hitter about facing Paul Byrd and they'll say, 'He doesn't back down . . . he challenges you . . . he keeps you off balance . . . you don't know what's coming next . . . the guy just knows how to pitch.' You could say the same thing about his writing style. From one chapter to the next in *Free Byrd* you'll be challenged, floored by his honesty, and inspired by his faith journey. The guy just knows how to write."

—Ernie Johnson Jr., sportscaster, TNT/TBS

"I started reading Paul Byrd's story and thought it would be a quick read. Forget it. I dropped everything I was doing and read it all in one sitting. Start reading and it'll happen to you. Make sure you've cleared a couple of hours. It's a life-changing book."

—Pat Williams,
senior vice president, Orlando Magic, and author, *Souls of Steel*

"I have been around professional athletes for nearly three decades, so I have to confess I was skeptical when I began to read Paul Byrd's story. But I was quickly drawn in by his unvarnished honesty and authenticity. Paul is as unorthodox in his writing as he is in his pitching delivery. He winds up and delivers the truth mixed with a really solid understanding of theology and grace."

—Dave Burchett,
Emmy Award–winning FOX Sports Network television director,
and author, *When Bad Christians Happen to Good People*

"Paul brings to *Free Byrd* the same spirit he brings to baseball, friendship, and life. He challenges conventional thought by always striving for authenticity, transparency, and truth."

—Tai Anderson,
bassist, multi–Grammy Award–winning Third Day

"*Free Byrd* takes you inside the clubhouse but even deeper into Paul's own heart. Paul Byrd might very well be the most genuine and transparent person I've ever met. His insights are truly inspired. You'll be recommending this book to everyone you know."

—Will Dawson, sports reporter, CBN's *The 700 Club*

"I have spent time in the locker room with Paul Byrd for a few years now. The thing I like most about him is that he treats Cy Young winners and laundry boys in the same capacity, with the love of Jesus Christ."

—Paul McKenzie, visiting clubhouse worker, Minnesota Twins

"I am a baseball fan, but I would have endorsed and recommended *Free Byrd* to all my friends if it had been written by a plumber. At its core, this book by Paul Byrd is about the journey of discovering and embracing an authentic and transformational relationship with Christ beyond the pat answers, simplistic formulas, and endless list of dos and don'ts, which is too often passed off as 'Christianity.' You won't be disappointed if you love baseball, but the gem of this book is discovering there is much more to knowing God than being good, doing church, and waiting for heaven when you die."

—Jim Palmer, author, *Divine Nobodies* and *Wide Open Spaces*

"I met Paul when I was co-chaplain of the Atlanta Braves. Paul helped me understand who I was in Christ. I am now free to live the Christian life, and thanks to Paul, that has energized my calling!"

—Mike McCoy,
Bill Glass Champions for Life, eleven years in the NFL

"Dad, why would anyone want your autograph? You're just average. If you were any good, the Yankees would have traded for you."

—Colby Byrd

FREE BYRD

THE POWER OF A LIBERATED LIFE

PAUL BYRD

HOWARD BOOKS
A DIVISION OF SIMON & SCHUSTER
New York   London   Toronto   Sydney

Our purpose at Howard Books is to:
- *Increase faith* in the hearts of growing Christians
- *Inspire holiness* in the lives of believers
- *Instill hope* in the hearts of struggling people everywhere

Because He's coming again!

Published by Howard Books
A Division of Simon & Schuster, Inc.
1230 Avenue of the Americas
New York, NY 10020
www.howardpublishing.com

Published in association with the literary agency
of Sanford Communications, Inc., Portland, Oregon,
www.sanfordci.com.

All author royalties for the sale of this book will be donated to the Byrdhouse
Ministries, which benefits various Christian children's and youth ministries in
the United States and abroad including orphanages and inner-city programs.

Library of Congress Cataloging-in-Publication Data
Byrd, Paul.
Free Byrd: the power of a liberated life / Paul Byrd. —1st ed.
p.   cm.
1. Byrd, Paul. 2. Baseball players—United States—Biography.
3. Christian biography—United States. I Title.
GV865.B7A3   2008
796.357092—dc22   2008006463
ISBN-13: 978-1-4165-8723-1
ISBN-10:   1-4165-8723-3

1   3   5   7   9   10   8   6   4   2

Manufactured in the United States of America

For information regarding special discounts for bulk purchases,
please contact: Simon & Schuster Special Sales at
1-800-456-6798 or business@simonandschuster.com.

Edited by Denny Boultinghouse
Cover design by Jeffrey B. Gibble/INDUSTRY
All photographs are courtesy of the author unless noted otherwise.

This book is dedicated to my wife, Kymberlee,
for her sacrifice and forgiveness over the years.
Thank you for seeing past my sins and
calling me a godly man when that's the last thing
I felt was true.

You are an amazing woman!
I love you.

CONTENTS

CONTENTS

FOREWORD

Christianity and perfection have a strange relationship.

I strive for perfection in baseball. In 1995 our team won the World Series, in 1996 I won the Cy Young Award, and I have made many All-Star teams. But as far as perfection goes, I have come up short and had games where I have struggled to get out of the first inning and found myself waking up after arm surgeries wondering if I'd ever pitch again. Regardless of how my arm feels or how good or bad I do on the field, there is always someone sitting in the crowd or hanging out in the press box taking notes and judging my performance.

In 1995 I acknowledged that I wasn't perfect and began a relationship with Jesus. But sadly, Christianity has felt a lot like the baseball field for me. I have strived for spiritual perfection and had many All-Star moments, but I have also had some bad games as a father, husband, and friend. Even though I signed up to have Jesus erase my failures, many people seem to want to point out and write down my mistakes.

I have been friends with Paul Byrd for almost twelve years now, and he has walked with me through some of the good and bad times, both on and off the field. I have always appreciated his honesty and the fact that he cares about me as a person and not just as a baseball player. He has reminded me that I need Jesus in my successes and my failures, and the only finger he has pointed has been aimed at God.

That's what I like so much about Paul's message. I don't feel like he's judging me or rehearsing where I've failed. And he's not giving me some five-step solution that worked for him and now needs to be applied to my life. When I read his writing, I am refreshed by his honesty and genuinely encouraged to see through my failures. I feel like we are sitting down at Starbucks while he shares about his own inadequacies—and how much God loves me in the midst of a broken world. After a conversation like that, I find myself focusing on God rather than any current pain or shortcomings.

At first, it might surprise you to see Paul taking on a book like this. Like me, most people know him from baseball. And if you went back and talked to some of his English teachers over the years, they'd probably be surprised to hear that he wrote this book himself. But just in case we need reminding, Paul shouldn't be a pitcher either.

I told Fox Sports this past summer that if he was a college pitcher today, he wouldn't even get drafted. But somehow Paul has managed to play professionally for eighteen years and stay afloat in the big leagues for twelve years. He makes his below-average fastball and goofy windup work against some of the greatest hitters in the world over and over again. Bobby Cox calls him one of the best he's ever seen at figuring out how to get guys out. And with his raw sincerity and under-polished language, Paul may be one of the best I've ever seen at reminding us just how much God loves us—no matter how much we might not deserve it.

If you look closely, this is not a book about baseball. It's not really about Paul's life either. It's about what it means to have a real relationship with God and not religion. It's about identity, grace, fatherhood, battling against sexual sin, Christian masculinity, accepting trials, and not using God. Most of all it is about the freedom and acceptance found in God because of what Jesus did for us on the cross, which somehow magically in His eyes makes us perfect.

John Smoltz,
lover of Jesus and
pitcher for the Atlanta Braves

If the Son sets you free,
you will be free indeed.

—Jesus Christ
John 8:36 NIV

BEATING RANDY JOHNSON
AND THE TROUBLE WITH DAVID

ONCE UPON A MONDAY night in August, I accidentally got to pitch in the big leagues. I buttoned up a red pin-striped jersey and threw a baseball for the Philadelphia Phillies. I was playing for the Braves Triple-A team at the time, and the Phillies purchased my contract off the waiver wire. I was supposed to be sent to Philadelphia's Triple-A team, but some crazy rule in the wavier process forced Ed Wade, the Phillies' general manager, to send me to the major leagues for at least a day. Because the Atlanta Braves minor league system had seen enough of my act the previous two years, they peacefully let me go with a handshake.

I will never forget that call.

After a few days of hanging out in limbo and holding hands with my overly calm wife in our cozy Richmond, Virginia, apartment, Mr. Wade called and said, "One of our pitchers got hurt yesterday. Congratulations, you're going to the big leagues." Then he chuckled and followed with, "You're going to get one start on Monday night against the Houston Astros and Randy Johnson. After that we have no idea what's going to happen."

I was in shock. My wife, Kym, was in shock. And as my two toddling boys, Grayson and Colby, pulled at my blue-jeaned pant legs, I realized that I had just gotten called up to the big leagues by some cosmic mishap—and in three days I was going to have a gun-slinging showdown with one of the greatest pitchers of all time. Confusion, joy, fear, thankfulness, anxiety, and all sorts of other claustrophobic emotional nouns seemed to take turns licking my brain senseless. Part of me wanted to compete and immediately grab a ball and hit the catcher's mitt to take down Randy Johnson and the Astros—and the other side of me wondered if this is what a man on death row feels like days before he's going to be executed.

On Monday, before I arrived at the stadium, Terry Francona, my new manager, asked a few players in the locker room what he should expect from me, but to his disappointment none of the hitters remembered facing some guy named Byrd. Nevertheless, Terry still decided to give me one start for my new team in hopes of seeing what I could do. My entire career was on the line that night and I tried to stay positive. I continued to fight back against the creeping feelings of fear and possible failure. The fact that I had to face Randy Johnson only made me take longer and deeper breaths.

Randy is a giant of a man who over the years has earned the nickname "the Big Unit." He stands about six foot ten with gangly arms and long legs that come flying at the hitter as his pitches sometimes reach the strike zone at around one hundred miles an hour. He is so tall that his body cuts down the distance to home plate giving his pitches the effect of a greater velocity than the simple numbered score of a radar gun. I had never seen a major league hitter literally fear a pitcher until the 1993 All-Star Game when John Kruk, a Phillies hitter, stepped out of the batter's box after one of Randy's pitches went sailing over his head. Kruk smiled a sigh of relief that the pitch didn't hit him and after a few more tense moments was happy to strike out and walk back to the dugout unharmed.

In 1998 the Big Unit began a four-and-a-half-year stretch of total dominance over the National League that the modern era of baseball had never seen before. He crushed and chewed up big-league hitters like a dog inhales treats. I sometimes wonder if he even tasted them. During this time, he amassed 91 wins, 1,533 strikeouts, a minuscule ERA, tons of innings, and a World Championship. Every possible statistical column that had to do with pitching was jaw dropping.

So in 1998, when the Phillies claimed me off waivers and gave me that fateful start in Veterans Stadium, not one single sportswriter gave me a chance to beat Randy Johnson. And they shouldn't have. To be honest, I was just happy that they spelled my last name correctly in the paper and actually mentioned that I would be pitching too.

I told my friend John Deatrick, a Catholic priest from Louisville, that I wanted to throw a shutout and beat him one to nothing. He said that he didn't have enough holy water in the state of Kentucky to make that happen and I should just go out and have fun.

When I did arrive at the stadium, Terry Francona was the first to shake my hand. Then he nodded and told me to "relax and have fun." Greg Jefferies, a new teammate of mine, started laughing when I made my way back to the underground bat room and picked out a smooth Louisville Slugger with someone else's name on it. He said, "I don't like your chances at the dish [home plate] tonight." Then he told me, "Pick a light bat and don't forget to go have some fun."

As I grabbed a smaller bat, I remembered Goliath, the giant Philistine champion from Gath, who stood over nine feet tall and walked in front of the armies of Israel chanting and screaming at them to send him one man to fight for their freedom. For forty days he strutted across a ridge with heavy armor and yelled, "I defy the armies of Israel today! Send me a man who will fight me!" Similar to my upcoming battle with Randy Johnson, where I had only one chance to prove myself, a great deal of me felt like the deeply shaken Israelites.

I smiled a rich grin when I thought of the words of David, the little brash red-haired shepherd boy who stood up for God, as I walked over to my new locker and read the story again. One of my favorite lines of the entire Bible comes from David who as a young boy says with regard to Goliath, "Who is this uncircumcised Philistine who dares to defy the armies of the Living God?"

When all the toughest men of Israel didn't want to get in the batter's box with Goliath, David did. He wanted to walk up to the dish.

David, in his youth, told King Saul, "Let no one lose heart on account of this Philistine; I am your servant and I will go and fight him."

The king of Israel responded, "You are not able to go out and fight this giant Philistine; you are only a boy, and he is a warrior who has been fighting from his youth."

Again, the boy replied, "When I tended the flocks of sheep on the hillside and a lion or a bear came and carried one off, I took my sling and went after it. Then I struck it and rescued the sheep from its mouth. When the lion turned on me, I seized it by its hair, struck it and killed it. Your servant has killed both the lion and the bear; this uncircumcised Philistine will be like one of them, because he has defied the armies of the Living God. The Lord who delivered me from the paw of the lion and the paw of the bear will deliver me from the hand of this Philistine."

Saul said to David, "Go, and the Lord be with you."

The giant Philistine Champion approached David on the battlefield and looked him over, seeing that he was only a red-haired little boy with flushed cheeks. Goliath despised David. "Am I a dog, that you come at me with sticks?" And the giant cursed David by his gods. "Come over here," he said to David, "and I'll give your flesh to the birds of the air and the beasts of the field!"

David said back to the Philistine, "You come at me with a sword and spear, but I come against you in the name of the Lord Almighty, the God of the armies of Israel, whom you have defied. This day the Lord will hand you over to me, and I will strike you down and cut off your head. Today, I will give the dead bodies of the Philistine army to the birds of the air and the beasts of the field, and the whole world will know that there is a God in Israel. All those gathered here will know that it is not by sword or spear that the Lord saves; for the battle is the Lord's, and he will give all into our hands."

When Goliath moved closer to attack the red-haired boy, David ran quickly to the battle line to meet him. Reaching into his bag, he pulled out a smooth stone and with his sling threw the hard rock perfectly into the forehead of the giant. Goliath fell facedown on the ground and David ran over to him drawing the Philistine's own sword from his scabbard and did what he said he was going to do.

5

I looked up from my locker and was still. I had no animosity for Randy Johnson; as a matter of fact I admired him. I didn't want to cut his head off, I just wanted to beat him on the hard Veterans Stadium Astroturf and get a chance to continue pitching in a major league uniform. For someone like me who had always been looked at as too short and not very talented, it was a big deal to get a shot at beating a legend in the making.

I usually don't pray to God asking for victories, trying to leave room for his sovereignty by asking him to live his life through me so that I might somehow bring glory to him through competing, but that day I prayed differently. No. Instead, I prayed hard that I would beat him one to nothing without holy water and without a metal sword. I feel I matured right there in front of my locker and grew past mimicking a rehearsed prayer where I said words I thought God wanted to hear. I felt hungry. I wanted a win and I asked him for it.

After strong and focused conversation with God, I pulled up my socks and took the field to do battle and have fun.

God answered my prayer. It was a yes.

I beat Randy Johnson that night four to nothing, throwing a four-hit shutout. The most unusual part of the evening came early in the game when I drove in the game-winning run by getting a hit off the Big Unit. I swung off the mark at what I thought was one of his fastballs but as I extended my barrel of grainy wood across the plate the ball broke sharply toward it and somehow ended up dancing through the air over the shortstop's head. I ran to first base in the midst of what felt like a dream as many cheering fans came to their feet. My first-base coach, Brad Mills, took my batting gloves from me with a smile.

"His fastball is unbelievable! I can't believe I hit it. It moves so much," I said between heavy breaths. I learned the next day that I had actually hit a hanging slider.

I walked to the plate in the eighth inning to a standing ovation while the theme song from the movie *Rocky* blared from the speakers. I laughed.

It was a magical night in the City of Brotherly Love, and I felt the realness of God and his work in our present-day lives among the so-called ordinary people who walk up against modern-day giants. It was a night that proved to be Randy Johnson's only loss in the National League that year and it came at the hands of a man with a big forehead whom no one gave a chance.

After the game, when the reporters asked me how I managed to pull something off that was so improbable, I responded by telling them about my prayer and the story of David. *USA Today* printed my words and I felt alive the next morning as I read them without getting one wink of sleep.

The truth is I have always related to David and stories about underdogs who face their giants. Although I have never desired to kill an agnostic for making fun of my Lord, I do feel a deep passion for God. And when I walk out onto the pitching mound and look at my surgically repaired arm, I feel like I am carrying some rigged-up slingshot that has to throw a perfectly placed pitch or I'll be the one who loses my head. Even off the field, I believe God will do great things through me, but when I look in a mirror or check my spiritual stats, I feel inadequate. I look somewhat short. Stupidly, I compare myself to amazing men like Billy Graham, Tony Evans, or Rick Warren and I feel weak. I seem to forget that God doesn't want another one of those men or they would have twin brothers and he is happy with me the way I am and with what I bring to the table, even if it's not very attractive.

I pause.

You know, God loves you and me the way we are, even with all of our sinful baggage and apparent incompetence. As I get older, the more I truly believe that it is when we are weak and vulnerable that God begins to work through us and sustain us with his grace. It's almost like he is showing himself off through a broken red pot to let other people know he can work through a mess and shine through anybody who is willing to rely on him. It is in these moments that we must smile and thank God for the various scars on our arms and in our lives that have shown us to be imperfect. We have to understand that there might be times when we will fall down spiritually or misrepresent God. And like the boy who fought Goliath, we must respond, get up, and wipe our snotty noses while saying, "Who is this uncircumcised Philistine?" We must do this even if the giant that seems to threaten our relationship with God feels like he lives within our very selves. We must face our adequacy in him. As it is written, "Even though a righteous man falls seven times, he rises again, but the evil are brought down by calamity." I think we should get up, regardless of who or what trips us.

The following afternoon, I walked into the Philadelphia clubhouse feeling like a hero. I walked over to my locker and found a large manila envelope sitting on my chair. It was thick, and I wondered if it was full of cheese steak certificates or something nice since I had pitched so well. It wasn't. To my amazement it was filled with Xerox copies of numerous articles that showed many older biblical characters and present-day Christians who had done horrible and atrocious things over the years.

David's slipup with Bathsheba was at the top of the list.

I looked at the cover of the envelope to discover that there was no return address or name on the outside and since it didn't have time to go through the post office, I knew it was an inside job, sort of a paper hit-and-run.

I found only a note among all of the pages with a few words saying, "Paul, I just want you to know the real character of the God you serve. He confuses people's language and causes them to fight and war against each other. He approves of innocent children being slaughtered as you can see from the Passover. He has let men over the years take hundreds of wives while the women had to be devoted to only one husband. He has sent fire down from heaven to destroy complete cities and turned people into salt for simply looking back in response to a few desperate noises. He even approved of the slaughtering of his own Son, who died on the cross. And now you come in here and brag on God's character as if he is someone that we should all become attracted to. You haven't the faintest idea what you are talking about. You are a fool. Sleep well my friend."

Although I wanted to send the skeptical masterpiece off for handwriting analysis, I stuffed my urge and just chewed on the words of this cynical detective. I knew I had quickly established myself as a Jesus Freak and I would have to answer questions such as these if I was going to be dropping pickup lines for God among my postgame comments. I prayed to understand the flaws of people who loved God and to make sense of these troubling observations.

A few years back, I had an ongoing written debate with an atheist who was a teammate and remains a friend to this day. It lasted about eight months. We passed our points of view back and forth, communicating our thoughts on a notebook. He demanded that I give him proof that God existed so I gave it to him.

I made a few masterful points and told him how penguins can jump six feet in the air and how sneezes zoom out of our mouths at speeds over six hundreds miles an hour, but these cold hard facts didn't really impress him very much. I was shocked. Therefore, I took a different route.

I told him, "Faith, the gift of believing that which is not seen, does not require us to coat check our brains at the door."

I continued by explaining the mathematical probabilities of fulfilled prophecies that present themselves in both the Old and New Testaments, which is something that has always amazed me. Then I followed with a lob shot and mentioned the minute percentage of literary variations in the manuscripts of today's scriptures and the Dead Sea Scrolls, concentrating on the fragment from Isaiah that was dated two hundred years before the time of Christ. As I suspected, consistent textual accuracy was important for him. I brought up the argument of intelligent design and tried to open his eyes to the ridges of God's fingerprints that are all over both the visible creation and invisible things as well.

Stubbornly, he rebutted.

I made a couple of more masterful points. Followed by some weak arguments from him. Then I gave an incredible speech on paper that Einstein couldn't refute. Then more nonsense from him.

I write these words with a smile.

I think the greatest thing that we both appreciated about our talks and paper discussion was the fact that we listened to each other.

Nevertheless, one day while volleying our thoughts back and forth with a pen, I learned that my friend wasn't really looking for proof of God and his existence. Instead, like my anonymous hit-and-run friend from Philadelphia, he was looking for evidence that God was *good*.

I found this out one day when he too brought up the trouble with David.

"And if I did believe in a god, which I don't, I sure wouldn't pick the one in the Bible. I mean look at David. He had sex with his friend's wife, got her pregnant, and then killed her husband. And what was your God's response to that? He called David a man after his own heart!"

Atheist John Doe had made a point to think about. It was one I had to consider.

Our discussions became even better after that exchange and I learned that at one time my atheist friend believed he was a Christian. Like most of us, my friend had deep struggles and embarrassing pain. And he prayed hard for God to change his troubling desires and take them away. When no one answered him, he decided that his Creator wasn't for him. My friend then chose to pretend as if God had never been real in the first place. He promptly got involved in a skeptics club and began to arm himself with arguments that set themselves up against the knowledge of God. He had joined the dark side of disbelief and rejected the goodness of the Almighty.

I really hope my friend has some type of Darth Vader last-minute conversion experience where he changes his mind. I hope one day soon his young son will help him take off that heavy black mask.

I once walked into a typical big building American church to speak on the love of God. It was the church's twenty-fifth anniversary so they had rented out a large auditorium for the event. It was ginormous. A large number of people attended, and I was a little intimidated being half the age of many people in the crowd. I felt as if the older faces knew it all and I didn't. What could I bring to the table in my youth? I hoped they wouldn't roll their eyes at me when I took the stage. I don't like it when eyes make circles.

The main reason I was the featured speaker was due to the fact that I was a current major league ballplayer with the Philadelphia Phillies. When the pastor introduced me, he talked of my character or at least my reputation in major league baseball and the community. He also talked of my family. Since he didn't have access to the entire closet of my life like God does, the introduction the pastor was giving to the crowd was very flattering. I sat there thinking and getting a little full of myself. Arrogance is always dangerous, especially when it starts to grab a hold of you just before you speak. If you don't recognize it, you might get up there and start preaching about yourself. And apart from him, we are all very boring and lifeless.

But then I thought of something. What if the pastor introduced me by saying that I was a great man of God and had done wonderful things for Jesus in the past but recently I had fallen into some trouble? Then he continued by stating that I had started an affair with one of my teammates wives. I had initiated having sex with her and gotten her pregnant. And since I was the chapel leader of my team and had a solid reputation, I needed to cover it up. So in an effort to do that, I called a friend of mine that was a hit man and had my teammate murdered.

What if the pastor then continued his introduction of me by further explaining that I had no control of my family? My son had slept with my daughter along with one of my wives and was now trying to kill me, his father. The video of my son lying intimately with my wife was now circulating the Internet and was available for anyone to see with just a few simple clicks of a computer mouse. I wondered if the crowd would listen to me intently after that kind of an introduction, or instead, would call the police.

Of course, I'm giving you a modern-day example of some of the sad mistakes and ending events of David's life. I have to confess now that I am thankful for people in the Bible like David. I think the Bible sends us messages that we can still love God even after we make crucial and horrible mistakes and it also lets us know that he can still speak through us despite our sins.

It's almost like God has the ability to make light shine out of darkness.

I think we sometimes judge maturity by looking at the number of visible sins in a person's life. But I think God is different from us when he says he looks at a person's heart. He judges a little more accurately than we do. And I have learned in life and through numerous scriptures that a person with a clean heart can do some pretty bad things. I think this is one of the reasons that there are no cover-ups in scripture. Outrageous behavior by people throughout the Bible is recorded and not compromised or deleted. The mistakes communicate to me that God will still take anyone who loves him or calls out his name.

Recently I picked up a book by Peter Kreeft called *Christianity for Modern Pagans*. It is basically a dissection of Blaise Pascal and his *Pensées*. The great French mathematical genius explained the importance of intellect and reason when coming to Christ but also warned us not to forget about the heart.

I learned that each of our lives is like a ship on open waters. We look at the stars and try to chart a course but God controls the waves. We reason with ourselves and scratch our heads trying to make sense of our journeys, wondering how the tides have brought us to the decision between heaven and hell. It is then that an honest man knows that the captain of the ship is his heart. And he has a choice to believe in God's way or his own, a choice to turn the rudder and aim for a heavenly city or a fading familiar world.

Kreeft picks up on Pascal by saying, "It is with our heart that we make the fateful choices of our God, our mate and our career . . . Therefore, our eternal destiny depends, not on our intelligence, which we largely inherited, but on our heart and will and love, which are freely chosen and for which we are justly responsible forever."[1]

I guess our hearts really do matter more than our heads, and even though we hunger for our actions to match our love for God and other people, I would be lying to say that it always turns out this way. Sometimes we are like children and yell at our stuffed animals instead of hugging them. Sometimes we take out our frustrations on the person we are the closest to and love the most. There is much in this world that makes me sad.

There was a time early in my walk when I misunderstood the Bible. I studied the Bible with my head, kind of like a textbook. I pored over the Psalms, studying them to take a final that wasn't scheduled. After a while, I got it. What I got was that I wasn't supposed to be doing that. I think the main reason all biblical books are written is to lead us into a relationship with the author.

Let me try to say it in another way. Instead of studying the Psalms with our heads, we should be writing them with our hearts. Penning our own. I'm not saying that we should never read the poems of the Bible or study helps; we should. I'm just saying that after a few good reads we should get the feel of what pleases God. We should look at how David interacted with God. It obviously pleased our Father. Was David honest? Did he follow a popular paperback of his day entitled, *The Ten Perfect Steps to Prayer*? Did he dance? Were his eyes closed while he was yelling at God? Did David bathe before he danced? Could it be that none of these things mattered and God just simply enjoyed being the top priority on David's heart list?

John Eldredge, the author of *Wild at Heart*, joked around one time at a retreat in Colorado saying that David might have had a multiple-personality disorder. He said this because David changes his tone and way of thinking so much throughout his writing.

I just thought David might have been a little bipolar and unable to run down the street to a doctor or local drugstore.

Listen to him in the Psalms.

"I am not afraid of the multitude of people who attack me from all directions. Rise up, LORD! Deliver me, my God! Yes, you will strike all my enemies on the jaw" (Psalm 3:6–7 NET).

And, "I will lie down and sleep peacefully, for you, LORD, make me safe and secure" (Psalm 4:8 NET).

And, "Listen to what I say, LORD! Carefully consider my complaint! Pay attention to my cry for help, my king and my God, for I am praying to you!" (Psalm 5:2 NET).

And here, I sometimes wonder if David is yelling at God or he doesn't understand how to use an exclamation point properly. The long sticks that stand over dots are all over the place. David writes, "I will thank the LORD with all my heart! I will tell about all your amazing deeds! I will be happy and rejoice in you! I will sing praises to you, O sovereign One!" (Psalm 9:1 NET).

In another psalm: "Why, LORD, do you stand far off? Why do you pay no attention during times of trouble? The wicked arrogantly chase the oppressed; the oppressed are trapped by the schemes the wicked have dreamed up. Yes the wicked man boasts because he gets what he wants; the one who robs others curses and rejects the LORD. The wicked man is so arrogant he always thinks, 'God won't hold me accountable; he doesn't care.' He is secure at all times. . . . Break the arm of the wicked and evil man!" (Psalm 10:1–4, 15 NET).

Just before I shake my head back and forth to make fun of David for acting like a kid on the playground, God reminds me that my head and heart think in the same way. I just don't tell God like David did. I just scratch the egg-shaped melon that sits atop my shoulders and ask myself, "I wonder why God always takes care of that guy?" And when I pray, I don't get emotional and yell at him to pay attention. I am too respectful for that. But I do raise my voice to my wife demanding that she hear me, and we are very close. Maybe I am the one who is confused. At times, my prayers lack intimacy. They lack passion. They lack exclamation points and question marks. Maybe I need to get more emotional with God like I do with Kym. I am real with my wife, even though I respect her. That's the way I want to approach God—opening up the depths of my soul to him, just like David did.

I guess the reality of the situation is that David was probably perfectly normal and the only one who was in touch with his true feelings. Either way I don't think that God cared. Or I guess he cared, I just think that God likes to be talked to more than he likes being talked about. And that's what the Psalmist did; he talked to God honestly.

As far as firsthand learning goes, I don't want my second son to study my first child's conversations with me over and over. I want my second son, Colby, to talk directly to me. He is different.

I believe that it is the same with God. We are all unique. I want to write about my own personal struggles and victories directly to my Father. Your psalms should be a little different from mine and unlike David's.

And like the biblical King David, we shouldn't be concerned with our enemies hemming us in. When David blessed his children while he lay on his deathbed, he didn't give them the ten steps to live by, he just simply took their hand and said, "Get to know your Father." I think he appreciated the process of learning from the Source.

POWERFUL!

One day recently, while sitting at an airport, I talked to a man who graduated from a top seminary in America. He had studied Hebrew and knew a great deal about the Old Testament. Because slender Bibles fit better in my travel bag, I asked him, "Why do the thinner Bibles have the New Testament combined with the Psalms and Proverbs? Are the Psalms and Proverbs theologically superior to the other Old Testament books?"

I guessed the book of Leviticus would not have been the best choice for an addition. It talks about the spilling of semen and unclean menstrual cycles.

He shuffled around the question, but we had a great discussion on the importance of Scripture. It was obvious that he knew a lot about the various books in the Bible. We talked a lot about the Psalms.

Then I asked him if he had written any poems to God.

"Poems to God?" he said with a question. "Why would I do that? You can't top the Bible."

It was a heartbreaking response. I think he had missed the point.

I know I am still a work in progress, but I think the life of David has really freed me in a way. I have learned that relationship counts to our Creator. It means more to him than the worldly scales most of us use to compare both our good and bad deeds against one another. God called David a man after his own heart before he defeated the arrogant giant named Goliath; before he became king; before his affair with Bathsheba. God said this about David while he was still a youth. All David did was sit by himself as a young boy and watch sheep while talking and singing to his heavenly Father. But then again most people don't do that. To most abandoned children, and that is what many of us feel like at one time or another, God doesn't absorb and consume their thoughts like he did David's. Most people would complain about why their lives were so unpleasant or why they had to sit alone for days on a hillside. Most people don't dance naked before him and write songs and poems of his goodness. Most people keep their clothes on because they care about what other people think and are afraid to get laughed at. I am ashamed to admit that I struggle to take the covering off my heart when I worship.

But not David. Again, he's nothing but trouble. And that trouble is why God announced to Israel and to us that he sought after and found, "a man after my own heart."

2

CHURCHILL DOWNS AND A DAMAGED LEFT TESTICLE

LOVE GOD.

I know my opening sentence is a little short. All in all, considering the time I spent proofreading, my first sentence took about seven seconds of this life to write down. But when I gazed at the brief ink tracks on paper, I realized that I would be agonizing in the good agony of loving God for the rest of my life, which means *forever*.

Speaking of forever, I *don't* believe that heaven lacks adventure or is a place where we lose our identity and become robots programmed to sound off at worship time.

I *do* believe we will be engaged in a deep, powerful relationship outside of time that allows us to give and receive love, to and from a person who cares more for us than any of our minds can imagine.

The truth is, my love was considered so valuable by God that he gave his Little Boy over to a torturous death in hopes of getting a little back from me. A friend once told me that if I were the only

19

sinner on the planet God would have still sent his Son down here for me in order that I might come home to him one day. I cried. After some thought, I decided that receiving love from God and throwing it back at him would be my mission in life, my very purpose. I want to give more of it. I hunger to love my Creator the way he deserves. But I struggle. And I have come to the conclusion that God will always deserve better.

I grew up in Louisville, Kentucky, and in our state people like horses, basketball, and whiskey. The Kentucky Derby is dubbed the best two minutes in sports. I think it is. As a kid I used to love going to Churchill Downs and watching the horses get sweaty as they ran down the backstretch struggling against one another. Horses are fierce animals that love to compete, and you could actually see veins popping out from their entire bodies as the perspiration flew from their silky coats while they gallop. I really liked when it had rained during the day causing their hooves to fling mud everywhere—all over themselves, the jockeys, and sometimes cheering fans.

One time, in the fifth grade, I saw a horse break his leg while he was coming around the final turn.

"Dad, what will happen to him? Will they put him in a cast?" I asked, having trouble picturing a horse wearing one.

"No," my father responded. "They'll have to put him down."

"What does that mean?"

"It means they're going to have to shoot him in the head, son."

"What?" I asked, while scratching mine.

I hunted down a trainer in the stalls after the day was over only to find out the horse really did have to be put down, the animal term for euthanasia. I wondered if the horse knew how serious things were as he hopped around on the track with a throbbing leg. The next day we went to Churchill Downs; the body of that horse lay under a yellow rubber tarp just inside the fence that was by the back entrance.

I wept.

My father taught me how to gamble properly. By the fifth grade I could read a racing form better than most bookies. My favorite horse was named Justin's Jellybean. He would break dead last stumbling out of the gate but somehow catch stride and muster up enough strength to catch the other horses in the end. I would scream at him as he crossed the finish line, usually coming in first.

"Go, Jellybean, go!" I would yell.

And I knew how to correctly place a wager at the box by that time as well. There is a special order of things, you know. You say the race number, the amount being wagered, the number of the horse, and the finish. I loved saying my rehearsed lines of gambling protocol to the older men who were seated behind the register taking my bet. It was kind of like ordering from the famous Soup Nazi from New York that was in *Seinfeld*. I would hand over a couple of green ones saying, "Race number seven. Two dollars. Number three. To win. Thank you, sir."

The more aged man at the ticket window would punch a few buttons, nod in approval, and hand me a little white piece of paper confirming the transaction. I would nod back and take my ticket as if it were some rite of passage into manhood. Sometimes I tried to walk away a bit, pretending to the onlookers as if I were on my own, as if I didn't know the man standing behind me was my father.

GAMBLING!

By the end of the summer, I had saved up fifty-five dollars from my winnings, which was enough to buy a pair of binoculars from the local Bargain Mart. This would allow me to get a better look at the horses breaking from the gate on the other side of the track, which was very important at that time in my life. Those are all great memories that still echo loudly in my head and are almost magical to me now. The binoculars still sit in my closet and I sometimes wonder if Justin's Jellybean is still alive grazing on long golden hay somewhere or chewing fresh Kentucky bluegrass in some distant field.

The truth is, I have always identified with horses running around a racetrack and felt like I was a part of them. A metaphor. My life has also consisted of competition, straining, and a little mud slinging. I have also identified with their pain. There have been times in my life where my heart has hurt and I would find myself hopping around not really knowing what went wrong or how serious things were. Brokenness. I guess I will forever be in the process of being completed and there are things in my heart that need to be confronted and put down too. Whatever it is, I've always felt so alive and engaged while watching horses race around the track.

Louisville Slugger makes baseball bats downtown near the river. They have a seven-story metal bat that leans against their building. It weighs thirty-four tons. It's officially the biggest bat in the world. And the heaviest. No one can swing it. It looks ginormous, as if it's going to crumple through the bricks at any moment. I think that watching a man or woman make a professional baseball bat is a must if you go to Louisville. Kids are especially mesmerized as the person uses a scraping tool, crafting the bat from a block of wood as it spins furiously on the lathe. Watching it get dipped after it's been sculpted into its special form is pure joy, even better than Dairy Queen. And then seeing the trademark burned into the wood. Then smelling it. Then picturing your favorite hitter swinging it and hearing the loud cracking sound. All magical too. I remember going on field trips as a young boy and watching the process. I had no idea I would be trying to miss so many of them with a stitched-up leather ball later on in life.

In Louisville I went to Sacred Heart Model School for my elementary education. Even though my mom, Lillie, called me handsome when she ran a comb through my hair, it was not a school for models. It was a Catholic school that was run by a bunch of nuns who cared about us. I don't think they were quite ready for me though, and I caused a lot of trouble. It used to be an all-girls' school. Because they had just started taking boys a few years earlier, my father said that they were still used to only girls.

I overheard him speaking to my mom one night from a room down the hall. "I'll tell you the problem right now," he said. "All the nuns want the boys to pee sitting down just like they do! That's what is wrong over there. They don't want anyone standing up at the urinal!"

I took his statement to mean the teachers wanted the boys to behave like the girls did. I think he really meant that the nuns didn't understand boys and were upset that he and my mother were called to the office quite often to discuss trivial things that he thought all boys did. Like teasing and fighting each other. Whatever the reason, I was very glad I graduated from that strict school and Sister Catherine didn't kick me out for causing such a ruckus in the classrooms and on a few of the grassy playgrounds.

Somewhere deep inside me I knew the teachers and sisters cared about me as a person and wanted what they thought best for me, and I found out later in life that in this world both love and concern are tough to come by. Looking back now, I see that their lives had a purpose—to shape and love children—which is very honorable. Again, I'm glad they had patience with me.

At Sacred Heart, I won a writing contest for young authors at our school. First place. I still remember blushing as the teacher read my story aloud to the class. I had a secret crush on a girl who often sat in front of me during my years at Sacred Heart and typed a romance novel about her that included us kissing on the beach. Thankfully, for privacy purposes, I changed her name, but I somehow forgot to change mine. It was sort of a Fabio-like love story, without the steamy picture on the cover. I definitely dropped down a few notches on the athletic coolness scale when the teacher delivered the romantic parts. I think my homeroom teacher knew this beforehand and read it in front of everyone to get back at me for talking so much and making her career so difficult. My guy friends were shaking their heads at me in disapproval. The girls were all smiling, laughing, and shouting, "Oooooh." To this day, those fifteen minutes were the longest of my life. I never thought my story would win. I thought that I would be undercover. That fateful day unquestionably left a mark on me for a while. A deep bruise. Later that year I got beat out in the state tournament by some sissy who wrote a book of poems, but that's a totally different story and I will not bore you with the details of that one. In short, I wanted to fight him for winning. I was in the eighth grade.

The following year, I attended a high school named St. Xavier. I made a friend that first semester named Devon who was a couple of years older than I was. Our school had a big-brother program, and I think he had missed signing up for it or something so he picked me up later without turning in any forms. I dated his girlfriend's sister, so it was easy for him to run by and pick me up on his way over to their house. I was not very good at making out though, and I assumed that this was the reason the little sister broke up with me.

On those drives Devon and I found out that we had a lot in common. We both liked music, basketball, and girls. I was a freshman on the basketball team and he was a senior. Devon actually had a good bit of stubble on his face and could have grown a full beard if he'd wanted to, so I thought he was cool. He also had spiked-up hair on the top of his head with a straight mullet dangling all the way down his neck. I think Billy Ray Cyrus copied him sometime later, so Devon got a perm on the end of his mullet to be different. He drove a pine green Ford Fairlane. We put some giant speakers that he purchased from Wal-Mart just above the backseat to impress the guys when we drove up to the basketball court for the pickup games. The speakers probably impeded Devon's vision when he looked out the rearview mirror, but he didn't care; the deep blaring bass was more important. I'm sure the odds were against us, and we looked like a couple of long shots riding up to the neighborhood basketball court blaring the song "Fly Girl." I would roll the window down and let my arm dangle over the side of the door. Thinking back, I don't know if we were hoping to look cool for the girls or trying to intimidate our round-ball opponents. But I guess it really didn't matter, because that's the way we rolled. We were actually pretty good. I would hit a jumper, point my index finger at him, and say, "What up, dog?"

My dad said we played the music so loud that he could hear the Fairlane coming into the entrance to our subdivision, which was about a half a mile away from our home. He said that I would be deaf by the age of eighteen. I thought that was also cool. You know, a battle scar from being a rebel.

The car was old and kind of beat-up. There was a large hole that had rusted out in the frame just beneath the passenger's floor-board. If you lifted the mat, you could see the pavement whizzing by beneath you. Since I am not Fred Flintstone, I had to be careful to put my feet up underneath the dash so I wouldn't get a severely stubbed big toe. It was my job when we were cruising at night to occasionally light a smoke bomb and drop it out of the hole beneath me as we drove through a major intersection. It took a while for me to learn the timing but after a while I thought I deserved some sort of military medal for being so precise and having such dead-on crosswalk accuracy. Or I deserved a ticket and some jail time; I guess it depends on how you look at it. We would circle back to check out the confusion, acting innocent as we pulled up to the haze of smoke that clouded the stopped cars at some random junction. I never made the connection that I could have caused an accident or gotten someone killed. We were young and we were stupid. I think one of the signs of youth is that you don't appreciate danger.

One time a policeman pulled us over and I had to ditch our contraband fireworks, which hailed from Tennessee. The only place I could find was a hole that we'd left under the giant speakers from our below-average installation job completed weeks before. I hopped over the front seat and quickly hid them. I felt like a professional hoodlum when my plan for stashing the goods worked.

Another night we stupidly walked into someone's driveway

to siphon gas because our tank was empty from cruising. I had never sucked gas from a tube before. All of a sudden the porch light came on, and I had a mouthful of what I think was regular unleaded. I learned that gas tastes terrible and breaking one of the commandments by stealing from your neighbor definitely has its drawbacks. We sprinted across a dark field that was behind the house carrying an empty gas can and six-foot hose. It's very hard to sprint across a piece of land covered in waist-high sage grass while carrying such incriminating evidence. Especially in the dead of night. I kept tripping over the hose, and Devon ran full speed into a wooden fence post that was hidden among the grass. It knocked him to the ground. I stood over him as he explained to me that he had damaged his left testicle really badly. Seconds later, he started to scream and roll around on the ground as the pain began to set in. He said later that he didn't cry but I think he really did. I am thankful we were not shot that night, leaving a trail of blood for beagles to follow.

It's funny how some types of pain register and others don't. If your left testicle gets whacked by a fence post, you pretty much feel it right away. But your heart can have a broken leg for years and you might not even realize it. High school was a fun time for me. But there was also part of me that was screaming and rolling around on the inside. I guess it just took a while for the pain to set in.

Devon went on to play hoops, disappearing to some small college somewhere up north. After a short college career, he returned to Louisville and worked toward becoming a pharmacist.

I liked the music in the eighties, the pop stuff, the continued British invasion, and my introduction to rap music, which featured LL Cool J. MTV played only videos then and I watched them while eating TV dinners on a tray in our living room. And when I stared at the television like I was in some sort of trance, I fantasized about growing up being somebody fashionable and important.

I had two baseball coaches during my days at St. Xavier. One named Dave Butler and the other Joe White. They lectured to students with pencils during the day, taught baseball to a number of us in the afternoons, and took turns driving a tractor until dawn trying to get the field ready for games. When we did have games only about ten people showed up. It was a thankless job but I realized how much time they spent with us. I also became aware of the smiles on their faces when we improved and understood more about the game.

I despised literature going into high school but soon understood the importance of opening a book. I had a great teacher named Mike Johnson who somehow made outdated literary works and poems about ancient life on Grecian urns absolutely fantastic. He had a wonderful sense of humor and was very passionate about the subject. Those rhythmic words came off the pages and made learning fun for me.

When the semester was over, I had learned a greater lesson from Mike and both of my coaches; a lesson greater than either baseball or the value of reading ancient poems. I learned that if you pursue your heart and do what you love, you will never truly have to work a day in your life. Instead, you will have fun and do what God has created you to do.

My other favorite class was art. I've always liked to draw even as a teenager. Miss Bowman was my art teacher and she would play music while we all sat around and did artwork. It was my first introduction to The Doors and eclectic seventies' music. There was no place that I would have rather been than in that art room. We all created and harassed one another about our projects as Jim Morrison sang mysteriously in the background backed up by an eerie-sounding organ. I even tried to forge my art teacher's name a few times on a permission slip to get in there during study hall when I should have been working on something else. It worked about ten times or so until I got busted, taken into custody, and ended up standing in front of a plain cement barrier for a couple of hours, courtesy of our detention program. Miss Bowman got really mad at me, and I found out that your standard classroom wall consists of 734 bricks.

I also admired a teacher named Dan Amlung at St. Xavier. He taught biology my freshman year. It was the first class of the morning and a student named Terry sat in front of me. The back of Terry's head was a deep reddish color and it wasn't as attractive as the girl who sat in front of me at the Model School. He always fell asleep after the first ten minutes of class because he had been delivering newspapers in the middle of the night while the rest of us slept soundly under our white cotton sheets. I felt guilty about that, like I was spoiled or something. I think Terry and Mr. Amlung cut a deal because he never woke him up. Since Terry sat between my eyes and the chalkboard, I did get a better view when he collapsed. The reason I liked Mr. Amlung had nothing to do with his teaching ability even though he was more than adequate. No, it was because every time he addressed us he called us men. The nuns at Sacred Heart did not do that and my mom called me honey, which I hated.

During adolescent years, if boys are addressed as men, something happens to them at the core of their being. When they sit there uncomfortably on the inside with zits, braces, and newfound hair growing all over them and someone calls them *men* it is like pure honey to their souls. It is something that, as a boy, you have been waiting for your whole life. All of a sudden the cracking voice doesn't matter and you walk forward as you are called out into masculinity.

I remember well Mr. Amlung sipping the morning's cup of coffee from his famed San Francisco Giants mug saying, "Listen up, men. Today we are going to learn about parameciums."

Ahhh . . . It was pure brilliance.

It was the mid-eighties and I drove to school in a gray Pontiac 6000 with a cool haircut that made me feel like I was in a band similar to A Flock of Seagulls. But I wasn't. Looking back now at old pictures, I'm not really sure what I was thinking. Maybe I was trying to be unique like my friend Devon. It still shocks me to learn that God loved me enough back then to work his fingers through the massive amounts of sticky hair gel and count the follicles on my head, even during the times in my life when I wanted nothing to do with him.

A few years later, I took some short story writing classes while attending Louisiana State University. I was laughed out of the class a couple of times on critique day. Although it hurt a little, I still tried to listen to other students' evaluations. I guess I always thought that my next story would be better. And I hoped it would get approval. But it didn't seem to happen for me. Maybe I should have gone back to writing steamy romance novels.

It all came to a crashing halt for me one day when the best student writer in the class exploded my final draft by saying, "This story sucks. Royally! It has so many problems I can't even critique it; I wouldn't even know where to begin!"

Everyone was quiet and no other student made a comment.

After the second hand of the clock slowly made its way past many notches the teacher spoke up and simply said, "I agree." I wanted to get up and leave but I didn't. Instead I just sat there feeling inadequate and embarrassed.

Young adulthood is a tough time to receive constructive criticism, especially if the analyst really doesn't care about you in the least. It was hard for me to admit it but deep down inside I knew he was right. My final drafts were pitiable. Nevertheless, I trudged ahead. I continued to take courses in various types of literature and writing.

That same year, for the first time in my life, I heard the hardcore version of the gospel. It was 1988 and I was seventeen years old. I was a freshman in college who was away from home for the first time with a new-wave haircut and a lot of cockiness.

One day in the press box at the baseball stadium, Wayne Waddell, a man with Campus Crusade for Christ, introduced me to the exclusivity of Jesus. I call it the get-off-the-good-guy program philosophy. He also talked about our eternal destiny, including heaven and hell.

Wayne asked me a tough question.

"Paul, if you died tonight and were standing in front of God and he asked you, 'Why should I let you into heaven?' what would your answer be?"

I told Wayne that God should let me in, "Because I'm a good dude and I didn't kill anybody." I said this while twirling an index finger through the back of my blond mullet.

He told me that when it came to getting into heaven, it really didn't matter what kind of person you tried to become, it only mattered if you asked Jesus to come into your heart. Immediately I had the feeling that this wandering self-appointed evangelist was possibly in a cult. Still, I could not get that message off my mind. It was an unfamiliar awareness, and I still didn't like it.

Growing up in Louisville, I had said prayers that I was taught to say like the Hail Mary and Our Father before I went to bed. Sometimes I tried hard to mean them by squinting my eyes a little harder and really focusing on what I was saying. And on occasion, I even said grace before big dinners like Thanksgiving and Christmas. I had never read the Bible for myself so I had trouble with what Wayne was saying. I was told my freshman year of high school that fundamentalists were weirdos. And it sounded like that was what Wayne was and at that point in my life I sort of agreed.

Nevertheless, I began to read a Bible that somehow appeared on a shelf in my college apartment. When I opened it, the pages stuck together. They were thin and crisp and had never been separated. To be honest, I still don't know how I came to own one. I read where it said, "God gave his only begotten Son that whosoever believeth in him should not perish, but have eternal life," and I thought to myself, *Whosoever believeth? Who talks like this?*

Miss Bowman and the nuns never talked like that. I reasoned that if God cared about me and his Son was the only way, wouldn't the Almighty come to tell me personally in my room on some random foggy night? Wouldn't he speak my language? And what about the guy in Africa who lived in a mud hut and never heard the gospel or some illiterate teenager who lived in the foothills of Kentucky? What about the cerebrally challenged? What about the people who lived before Jesus? What about children who die? What about dogs?

To be honest, the scriptures bored me and seemed outdated. I felt like I was in history class reading some ancient document that was no longer applicable to this world and was pretty much void of life.

After I put my Bible down for a week or so, I saw a movie called *Hellraiser*. It was a story about some people who were trapped in hell and couldn't get out. This was the place that Wayne had warned me about. There was a really scary guy in the movie who had a bald head, which was painted totally white. He also had sharp needles sticking out from his skull and a face with a gridlike pattern. One nice guy in the movie who was trying to escape the horrible-looking creatures got caught and was suspended in the air by large fishhooks that dug into him and held him up for what I guess would be all eternity or forever. I use these superlatives because I knew that he wasn't getting down on his own and everyone left him. I remembered thinking that if Wayne, the cult member, was right, then I was in trouble. Escaping hell is not the best reason to contemplate Jesus but I guess it is better than nothing so I began to sit awake at night and think about these things. I began to read the outdated words again and try harder to make sense of it all. I couldn't.

After more reading, the biblical issue that I struggled with the most was the fact that many nice people could end up separated from God, hanging out in a torture chamber for all of eternity. This sounded a little overdone to me. Judge Wapner from *The People's Court* would never have handed down such a harsh sentence to people who tried to be good. I mean the just man with a sleek wooden gavel whom I watched on television while growing up would never have ordered nice people who had visited children's hospitals on Sundays or people who care about their families to forever hang out with the evil man from *Hellraiser* just because they didn't ask God to forgive them through the person of Jesus.

Ouch! I mean, couldn't Jesus just burn them for a little while? You know, singe them a bit with a yellow Bic lighter or hold it under their index finger until they asked for forgiveness? It also meant that a lot of my family members would probably end up roaming aimlessly through that same fire for a long, long time while I feasted at the big table with Jesus and a bunch of other criminals like Jeffrey Dahmer, a cannibalistic serial murderer, who decided to fire up a last-second, all-cleansing prayer just as the buzzer was about to sound. I had never heard my relatives talk about Jesus personally so I wondered who in my family just went to church on Sunday for casual religious purposes and who really sat in the pew loving and thinking about God. I knew that I usually tried to scout out good-looking girls during the services while hoping that my mom would elbow me to signal that we were leaving early to beat the parking lot traffic jam.

All of these new ideas about God and heaven ran across my brain, leaving a trail of questions that bothered me and I wondered whether or not I should get out the phone book and call the nearest asylum. These were all very tough concepts for someone like me to swallow, a person who was content to try to be morally decent. I wanted to reject Jesus for deep emotional reasons that included my family, nice people, and common sense. But I also didn't want to go to hell. And that's when it hit me. I exposed a minor flaw in the gospel and discovered that I could just say a prayer to accept Jesus and sort of try him out like a new coat. If he didn't fit, I could just bring him back. And if my new friend Wayne, the one who was into it way too much, was right then I would be covered. If he was wrong, no harm done. I had just wasted a few syllables on a faulty fire insurance policy. I supposed that there was nothing wrong with being a little bit gullible. I mean, the world has bigger problems. Right?

I sometimes wonder if that philosophy is faith or not. Probably not.

Nevertheless, I said a prayer to dodge fire and verbally asked Jesus to come into my heart. I told him that I was sorry for living my life apart from him. I tried to mean it. And I asked him to be the one that saved me and not my good deeds. It felt very strange to me when I said an unrehearsed prayer to a physically invisible person whom I somehow sensed was sitting right there with me. I felt like I was talking to Harvey the Rabbit only his name was Jesus.

I had no idea that I was going to fall in love with Jesus shortly thereafter. The more I got to know him the deeper I fell. It sounds so weird to say that you have fallen in love with God as if he's personal and you go out for ice cream together. But that's what happened. Somewhere among the pages, I stopped reading the Bible like a textbook to gather information and I got involved in a profound meaningful relationship with the Author, one that could not be fathomed or truly explained by my rational head. I started talking to him and listening with more than my ears and he absorbed me. When I read, I began to learn of his kindness and enjoy how he handled conflict. I found myself lapping up stories that my eyes had run across before but had never really appreciated.

When the Pharisees brought the woman caught in adultery to Jesus, asking if they should stone her as the law commands, he doodled in the sand. Then he said, "If any one of you is without sin, let him be the first to throw a stone at her" (John 8:7 NIV).

Awesome. This was not the strict judge I thought that I knew. This was not the person that I thought went around pointing fingers at others' imperfections.

In the seventeenth chapter of John, a few chapters after Jesus called me his friend, I read where he prayed that God, his Father, would reveal to me the depth of his own love for me. It is written that God, the Father, loves me as much as he loves his Son, Jesus, which became very baffling to me. I was going to question God on this but I remembered his pep talk with Job and that made me scared. I remembered that I too was nowhere to be found when he stretched out a tape measure and marked off the dimensions of the earth's foundation. And I was not there when he comforted the deer in the woods and so I figured that I had no business doubting his love for me. He had done more than enough on Golgotha to demonstrate his heart toward me, so I shut my lips and kept my ears and mind open to his counsel. Again, I listened.

I think it's easier to listen to somebody when you find out that he loves you. He was not the judgmental critiquer that I somehow felt he was. The more I look back on my life I really believe that I had wanted to believe in a God who liked me from the very beginning. I think for a long time I confused God with the man who stood over that horse holding a gun to his head because he couldn't perform anymore. What I began to learn from the Bible is that God is into people with real problems who care about him and not men and women who put on fake religious masks and think that they are better than everyone else. For some reason I had missed the real God of the scriptures and bought into the world's system of man-made religion. Getting to know God better was and still is a tough process for me but one that is very worth it. Like David, I have enjoyed getting to know my Father.

So I let Jesus in those final years at Louisiana State and the fog of a fake purposeless life began to fall away. There were times when I cried harder than I did for the dead horse that was under the tarp. I felt like everything I had done prior to asking Jesus to enter my heart was meaningless. I felt as if I were carrying on with a life hitched up to some sort of Matrix-like machine that I wasn't aware of until someone approached me with the truth.

I also struggled with sin a great deal during those early days of walking with Jesus. As an athlete so much of my identity was based on my performance and when I couldn't live perfectly like I thought I was supposed to as a good Christian, I felt I had let Jesus down. Because I could not stop sinning, I kept trying to say the formal prayer to receive Christ over and over again, wondering why it seemed to take for only a few days. Those were tough years in their own unique way. Doubting my salvation. I loved the new Jesus that I had come to know but I felt like a hypocrite due to my poor behavior and I questioned when or if I could cut it. I often thought that the victorious Christian life might be way too difficult for me. I strived to keep quiet and get my own answers. I felt like the Outlaw Josey Wales drifting off into the sunset hungering to do it my own way all by myself. Sad to say, I was really like a baby crawling across a busy expressway. I needed help. I needed community and a spiritual mentor to build into me and care about me.

That's why I kept getting out my little yellow *Four Spiritual Laws* book, the one that Wayne gave me, trying to understand the formula for accepting Jesus a little more each time. I even baptized myself in a small motel room once while playing Double-A baseball, thinking that a lack of water might be my problem. I am not sure of heaven's official rules of baptism but I now realize that God had to be smiling. Eventually, I felt in my heart that God said the word "Uncle!" in the hope of getting me to give up and stop asking for something that I already had.

Now that I'm further along on my journey, I really believe that the first time that I even had a thought of wanting Jesus I became a Christian. And if my lips said it on a Friday, God had already done most of the work in my heart on Thursday. And the thoughts of being damaged, like Devon's testicle or the throbbing leg of that unfortunate warrior horse, gradually began to subside. So I learned to trust that as a Christian, I would probably have times where I would sin, causing me to need Jesus. But I would also have times of joy and victory causing me to lean on him as well. I guess I was beginning to understand that I was a project who would always need to rely on Jesus through the good times, the bad times, and better yet, as my very life. Because it took a while for me to understand that my salvation was not dependent upon my performance, I've just never been able to pinpoint an exact date when I accepted Jesus.

One time I smiled while watching *Larry King Live*. Anne Graham Lotz was being questioned about coming to know Jesus. Larry asked Anne when she became a Christian. She couldn't give him a time frame, date, or even tell him a year.

Gasping, Larry asked her, "Anne, then how can you be sure that you really are a Christian?"

"Well, I love Jesus," Anne responded.

Because I have experienced what Anne has, I thought that was a great answer.

3

THE GREAT DIMAGGIO AND
THE CHRISTIAN SUBCULTURE

WHEN IT COMES TO TIME, I hate how it flies. Then again, sometimes I enjoy its passing. I guess it depends if I'm making out with my wife or hugging the toilet thanks to some twenty-four-hour stomach bug. Regardless of my condition, there is a spiritual message in the slow and steady ticks of the clock high up on my wall.

My time.

During my appointed time of college, our baseball team at Louisiana State won the national championship. It was my junior year and after the last out we all ran onto the field and jumped on top of one another. We looked like a pack of stray dogs tearing into a tossed-out piece of meat. Chris Moock, our third baseman, got up from the pile with blood running down his face. One of the other players had unintentionally landed a metal cleat on top of his head.

I remember walking back to the dugout after our victory celebration on the dirt mound. I was told that winning a national title would be the greatest experience known to man and a personal accomplishment that no person could take away from me. Even at death.

Wayne, the cult member who led me to Christ, was standing beside the dugout and I greeted him with a hug and gave his two-year-old son Brant a high five.

"How do you feel right now?"

"I'm pretty disappointed," I said. "I feel empty. I guess I thought it would feel a lot better."

Wayne smiled at me as if he knew that the things of this world would never quite fill my heart as they once did.

I had worked for three years to celebrate on that mound in Omaha, the site of the College World Series, and although I was thankful and stuck my finger up in the air to give the number-one sign, for the most part, I still felt vacant. I wanted a refund. Maybe it was Jesus. Maybe it was the fact that I enjoyed putting sweat toward something that was now accomplished and I knew I had to move on. Whatever it was, I really wasn't sure. It was a strange emotion.

Our team traveled back to Baton Rouge where a sold-out stadium of raving fans welcomed us. It was the first national title for Louisiana State Baseball and the crowd roared as an announcer introduced us one by one. Armando Rios's name was called just before mine and he did a running backflip that would have made the famous Bart Conner proud. It was a perfect ten. Feeling a little sheepish following him, I did a cartwheel and almost broke my neck. Everyone laughed.

The real celebration, however, took place months later when our team visited the White House and I got to shake hands with President George H. W. Bush. Joltin' Joe DiMaggio and Ted Williams were also present. It was the fifty-year anniversary of their respective streaks. DiMaggio had hit safely in fifty-six consecutive games and Ted Williams was the last person to have a batting average above .400 when in 1941 he batted .406. Both missed time in the majors fighting in World War II shortly after that year. Not only did I appreciate them as baseball players but I was also very thankful that they went to battle for our country so that my children would not be speaking German or living under a dictatorship.

After President Bush said a few words recognizing each of our accomplishments, we all had our picture taken together. There were a lot of beefy men standing around us with sunglasses and curious-looking lumpy dress coats. I don't think they wanted us dog piling the president like we did our pitcher in Omaha, so our team remained calm.

I stood near the end of the middle row and Mr. DiMaggio walked over and positioned himself to my right. A lot of thoughts ran through my head as the cameras made clicking noises. I was standing next to one of the greatest sports heroes in the history of baseball, and a man who once caressed the face of Marilyn Monroe, one of the most recognizable movie stars of that century.

I had just read *The Old Man and the Sea*, a masterful work by Ernest Hemingway. I remembered his captivating words describing the elder fisherman, Santiago, as having a leathery neck, blistered cheeks, and hands that were permanently scarred from holding on to the rope he used to pull in his large catches. After a day of fishing, the Old Man encouraged Manolin, a young boy whom he was mentoring in the art of fishing, not to lose hope in his favorite baseball team.

"Have faith in the Yankees," Santiago said. "Think of the great DiMaggio."[1]

I also thought of the Simon & Garfunkel song, "Mrs. Robinson" and the lyrical question, "Where have you gone, Joe DiMaggio?"

I wanted to call the famous singing duo and tell them that I had found him. The long-standing icon of American history, the Great DiMaggio, was standing right here. Right here with me!

When we were done, I asked Joltin' Joe to sign a baseball for me. It was the baseball from my first professional win. I was drafted by the Cleveland Indians that year and had begun playing on their farm team immediately after the College World Series. Ironically, my first victory came against a Yankees farm team a few days earlier and I couldn't think of a greater name to grace the smooth leather that rested between those red seams. He pulled out a shiny chrome pen from his silky Italian suit and gave me his best signature. The Great DiMaggio was getting older now and his hand quivered a little as he began to write his name so he took a little extra time and gave me his best.

I knew while standing there fixed in that moment that the flesh of men really is like the green grass of a field. The blades are strong one day and wilted soon after. And our glories are like that of flowers.

When the Great DiMaggio found out I was playing with Cleveland, he encouraged me by saying, "Maybe you can help that team win a championship someday."

"Yes, sir," I said as if standing at attention. "I'll do my best."

I looked over at Ted Williams and the cowboylike turquoise choker that held his collar tightly together. I felt like I was looking at John Wayne or something. At this time, his frame was much sturdier than DiMaggio's and he stood with extreme confidence while shaking hands with thick steady fingers. I shook his right one wondering about the five years he missed during the prime of his career while the last great World War took place. I thought of old-time highlight reels, his beautiful fluid swing and I wondered what the crack of his bat sounded like just before he glided around the bases in Fenway Park to a crowd of wicked screaming fans. The Splendid Splinter.

I turned my eyes upward and watched the American flag wave back at the wind as it made a few rippling noises and I thought of the trouble in this world, the Gulf War and my emptiness over continued worldly searches. I was experiencing what King Solomon, the author of Ecclesiastes, wrote a few thousand years ago when he said that, "God has made everything beautiful in its time. He has also set eternity in the hearts of men; even though they cannot fathom what God has done from the beginning to the end." I found it confusing that God had put something in my heart that could not be fully understood by me, a mere man living in the confines of time on this earth. My heart and my head seemed to just be still and wonder at the works of God that were always there but, for some reason, were being made apparent to me now.

Later in the day, I returned to my minor league team knowing that God had been crafting my life with an invisible lathe or heavenly tool like the goggled man used in the back room at the Louisville Slugger factory. I remembered as a young boy watching scraps of wood fly at his mustached face while he worked his sharp metal instrument up and down the bat. Somehow, years later, I knew that I too was a work in progress like that rough piece of grainy ash. I could literally feel someone else living inside of me, refining my thinking and talking to me with thoughts that I couldn't ignore. As the shavings of my life flew, deep revelation covered me and spiritual truths that I would have otherwise had no way of knowing came to light. I also wondered if I would leave any green edges of fading glory on the baseball diamonds of men. And I questioned if, when withered like the Old Man of

Hemingway's masterpiece, I would command an autograph from an eager young fan.

I wanted to know that even if someone did want my autograph later on in life whether or not that would truly fulfill me. Because the College World Series didn't fill the hazardous dip in my heart and now after seeing the effects of time on American heroes of yore, I wondered if anything done on the bright stages of this world had a chance to satisfy me. Maybe a dazzling career in large stadiums full of people wouldn't satisfy the deepest longings in my heart after all. I began to believe that an honest relationship with God was the only thing that would really matter and stand forever. Even though Jesus had already entered my heart, I still felt the pull of the weeds and worldly things growing around me and presenting me with daily options of which master to serve. Baseball had become more than just a game for me; it was turning into a spiritual battle.

SHAPING

There was a sadness to the Great DiMaggio on that sunny day at the White House. I didn't know if it came at the hands of nostalgia and the remembrance of days roaming centerfield in the Bronx or something else. I read some summers later where he stepped up at the death of Marilyn Monroe and protected her while arranging the funeral. Even though they were no longer married, I think her death really hurt him. He had a dozen roses delivered to her crypt two times a week for twenty years and he never talked of her publicly, nor did he ever marry again. That was sad for me. I suppose that even the most celebrated best-lived lives here on the playgrounds of men have many moments of deep pain.

Years after that day at the White House, I had a conversation with a young woman who worked in the media out on the West Coast. Although her face didn't get the same recognition throughout the world as Miss Monroe's, she had dated a lot of athletes and her features had become very familiar among the players in our league. As one of my teammates remarked, she was eye candy. The young woman interviewed me next to the field one day and when the camera stopped recording she had a very saddened face and asked me if we could talk. Because my wife and I have boundaries with members of the opposite sex, especially good-looking ones, I asked her to tell me what was wrong right there in the dugout, a place that was out in the open and safe.

She explained to me how she was raised in a Christian home and walked with God for about ten years starting in high school. She went to church, read her Bible, and even occasionally talked about God with a few of her friends at youth group. But her real passion was sports. She told me that her dad would take her to all kinds of sporting events and they would cheer, laugh, and intentionally throw popcorn on each other every time their team would score. Then, out of nowhere, her dad got cancer and died.

"After that, I gave up on God," she said with softness. "I can't understand how he let the one person that was so dear to me die so quickly. I barely got a chance to say good-bye. He'll never walk me down the aisle or hold one of my children. I miss him so bad."

"Did you have a strong relationship with God before your dad died?"

"What do you mean?"

"Well, it sounds to me like you had a great relationship with your dad. Apparently, he spent a lot of time with you and you guys had a lot of fun. As far as God goes it sounds like you might have only known about a bunch of rules to follow or some sort of life-style that consisted of good things to do. I'm not saying that you didn't have a relationship with God; I'm just saying that it might have been a little less than what it could have been or maybe should have been."

"Keep talking."

"Well, I mean the gospel is about relationship. A connection to God made possible through the suffering death and life of a Son named Jesus. I don't understand everything about God and the Trinity and I don't want to sound chauvinistic but the Holy Spirit appears to have a lot of characteristics that come naturally to a woman. Things like communication, comforting, and coun-seling. God the Father also claims to be a Spirit and has a lot of uniqueness and qualities of a father. After believing in Jesus, God the Father even asks us to address him as Papa when we talk to him. Even Jesus, in all his greatness, was constantly slipping off to spend alone time with his Father. And when Jesus resurrected, his first words were spoken to two women and he said, 'I am return-ing to my Father and your Father, to my God and to your God' " (John 20:17 NIV).

"I understand what you are saying to me and I know the gospel is true but I really don't care. God seems like a jerk to me right now. I don't understand how he can be so good and allow everyone to suffer. He wants credit when things go well. He wants praise. But when things go bad, he wants none of the blame. It's my fault or sin's fault or Adam and Eve's fault."

"Well, maybe you should ask him," I said.

"What do you mean?"

"That's exactly what I am talking about."

"What does that mean?"

"I mean that you don't know how to throw popcorn at God."

"What?"

"Look. What I am saying is that you knew your earthly father as a person. You talked to him. I am so glad that you came to talk to me and I will recommend someone if you like who will walk through this with you. But regardless of the person that you get advice from, you are going to have to start talking to God again and begin reading the Bible with the purpose of knowing him and not following a system. You're going to have to take your questions to God yourself. I'll bet you shared your feelings with your earthly dad and hugged him. I'll also bet that you had disagreements with him and you let him have it. I'm sure there were times when you just sat in his presence and were comfortable that he was in the same room as you but you didn't say a word. Am I right?"

"Yes."

"So now, you must learn to do the same with God. I know that you are considering God or you wouldn't have sought me out with tears. But now you can't reconcile the fact that he is good because he allowed you to be hurt. You're angry at him. So tell him! And ask him questions. I can tell you how he resolved that issue for me but he may resolve it in a different way for you. So ask him to show you. Talk to him like you did with your father. And I'll bet after you get things patched up you will learn, in a figurative sense, how to start throwing popcorn at him too."

"But he doesn't talk to me like that."

I sat quietly and didn't say a word.

"I think he just said something."

"Okay," I said. "That was quick. I'll be leaving now." I started to walk away when she stopped me.

"Paul, I'm not sure if I was ever a Christian."

"That's okay," I said. "I think I might have faked it for a few years myself."

I am not a psychologist, but I really believe that she had made herself available to these baseball players because it was the arena where she had connected emotionally with her earthly father. Once he was gone I think she hung around athletes possibly even wanting to marry one to fill the void left by the death her father. I walked away knowing that experiencing God was the only thing that would satisfy her deepest desire. I tried to point her to God. I also put her in touch with another female who I knew could continue the process of encouraging her to walk with God. I think she appreciated the fact that I didn't want to spiritually connect with her through her pain during her time of seeking. I think she had enough men who wanted to connect with her and most of them for all the wrong reasons. Although I have not seen her in recent years, I really hope that she either decided to begin a relationship with God or had her eyes opened to his goodness and continued onward in the one she already had with a better understanding of his character. Again, it's a lot easier to talk and listen to someone when you know they deeply care about you. I really believe that every creature under the sun needs to experience God's goodness.

Like King Solomon said, everything is meaningless apart from remembering and following your Creator. And that meaninglessness is not limited to bad things either. I believe doing good things or adhering to some religious system apart from God will also be insignificant when the lady with large lungs starts to sing and this world comes to a fiery end.

Blaise Pascal once wrote, "There is a God-shaped vacuum in the heart of every man which cannot be filled by any created thing, but only by God, the Creator, made known through Jesus."

I agree with the great French mathematician. This life is about receiving and experiencing God, the Heavenly Person.

One night, on a road trip to San Francisco, I had a heart to heart with one of my teammates in a shady local bar. He said that he really needed to talk to me about Jesus so I walked with him along the sidewalk and followed him down a flight of stairs into some hazy dark place so he could share his burden. I guess it was kind of like *Saving Private Ryan* only he wasn't a private and his last name wasn't Ryan. I wanted to talk about Jesus too and didn't want to miss the opportunity. So we sat down at the bar and he broke out a couple of fancy labeled cigars and insisted that I try a dark spicy one from the Dominican Republic. I'm not sure but I think he picked an illegal one from Cuba and lit it up. I didn't ask any questions and just sat there. He looked like a regular aficionado smoking his extra-thick tobacco roll. I mainly just coughed a lot and prayed that God would protect me from throat cancer. Not real smooth looking. Anyway, we had a great talk.

He started the conversation off by explaining why Jesus didn't work for him or better yet as he said, "didn't jive" with him. He said that he grew up in a Christian home and learned about going to church, tithing, quiet times, keeping sexually pure, witnessing, scripture memory, controlling his tongue, and prayer before supper. He was enrolled at a Christian school and was well educated on the theory of intelligent design and the story of Creation. His family dressed conservatively, acted properly, and talked about God a great deal. They even went to a soup kitchen a couple times a year where they volunteered to feed the poor. My teammate loved baseball and as time went on it became apparent that he was major league material. Even though he was drafted professionally, he ended up choosing to play baseball for a division-one university instead, putting his sports career on hold. It was at this university setting that he stopped watching reruns of *Leave It to Beaver* and exited his comfortable happy dome of cultural Christianity. He met other students who felt differently about the holy words of Scripture, and he listened to lectures by professors who ripped apart the Bible explaining why evolution was a much more accurate theory. He'd met with a Christian group on campus but said that most of the students sat around and made fun of and judged people for not being like them. He was saddened and turned off by their attitudes. After a time, he slowly began to side with the professors, feeling somewhat betrayed for having never been shown anything other than the religion of Christianity and discouraged that his Christian friends didn't love people like he thought they should have. He also felt that his parents had basically brainwashed him and had never given him the chance to make any spiritual decision for himself.

By the end of his junior year, he continued his path, traveling down every trail of the dark side he could find by getting involved with many different types of illegal drugs, experimental sex, and hard liquor. His loving Christian earthly father disowned him and they didn't communicate for years. After bottoming out and becoming discouraged by the fact that doing anything he wanted wasn't all it was cracked up to be, he decided to give the religion of Christianity one more shot. So he stopped cursing, stopped abusing drugs, stopped having weird sex, and stopped using alcohol. He began to pray before meals, have quiet times, memorize scripture, give money to a church, and actually witness to people about Jesus.

He purposely looked for and found what he called a "good girl" to spend time with and they stayed sexually pure. Because he was about to physically explode, he asked her to marry him and put a ring on her finger setting a date almost immediately. After nine months of marriage, they had a little girl. His world came to a crashing halt when he realized that he was acting a certain way solely to please his earthly father by cleaning up his life. Although he did so, he was still very unhappy. He really didn't want to do the things he was doing for God, but he did want some kind of morality in his life. He also became conscious of the fact that he had picked a wife who was like his mother instead of someone he truly loved and had a connection with. Now involved in an affair, he wanted to get a divorce and start all over again with a girl who he felt was a lot more like the real him but since he had a daughter and his wife was a nice person, he felt trapped.

He was so angry that Christianity had messed his life up that I began to wonder if he had brought me to the dungeonlike tavern in order to have me knocked off by some guy who worked for the mafia. I started to question whether or not he really wanted my thoughts at all. So I just sat there and kept listening.

"That's why it doesn't jive with me!" he said, almost breaking a beer bottle over the counter. "After all the things I gave up and all the things I started doing, you would think that Jesus would come through for me and make me happy."

"Really?" I asked.

"Yes, really! I mean why didn't he make it happen for me? I did everything I was supposed to. I turned my life around. I followed him. I said I was sorry to my family for hurting them. I even brought three people into the Kingdom. And what am I left with? Emptiness and misery all over again. I don't even love the girl I'm married to and now I feel like I'm living with my mom."

"Hmmm . . . ," I said. "During this time, did you ever . . . like . . . think about becoming a Christian?"

"What! Are you on drugs now? Did you hear anything I just said?"

"Yes, I did."

"Then what in the world are you talking about?"

"I guess I was waiting for you to tell me how much you loved Jesus despite the pain and trouble of this world. How much you feel his love for you. I have been waiting for you to tell me about how you talk to him as you go about your day and hear back from him through the whispers in your head and the tickling of your inner spirit. I wanted to hear how you noticed him during some of the times while hanging out with his people. I guess I wanted to hear about him and not some common religious system that some men have taken from the Bible in order to feel safe from the world and look good in the streets. It sounds to me as if you might have been acting like a modern-day Pharisee. Having religion and not relationship."

"Okay," he said with a hint of confusion.

"I am not saying the good things you did are bad, I do some of them too. I'm just saying that your motivation and source for doing them were wrong. It was for yourself and your earthly family. The Bible is not a self-help book or lifestyle to be lived. It is a large sign dressed up in ink that leads people to a greater reality. And that greater reality says that anyone who wants to engage can have a dynamic relationship with the Author. It is a book that expresses the concern of a God who wants to be your Father so badly that he gave his Son's life to redeem you. He might not get you out of all of your worldly trouble but he will sit with you among your problems and become the very solution to them. As a matter of fact the Bible says that in this world you will have trouble but you should take heart because he who is with you has overcome the world."

My friend was speechless for a good while. We smoked. He inhaled. I didn't. I soon got up and went to the bathroom to run water over my eyes that were now bleeding from secondhand smoke. As the water trickled over my pupils, I prayed that I had represented God accurately. After a few minutes I returned to my stool.

He continued, "Well, I guess if you put it that way, I was never a Christian in the first place. It's true. I've never had any real interaction with God in my entire life. As a matter of fact, I basically faked it to make my family happy with me. Like you said, I'm part of some religious system."

"Okay," I said.

After some silence and a few small smoke rings, he asked me, "So what now?"

"You might ask God to interact with you. But only if you want to. You might find that Christians like me are a little banged up but God isn't. He loves people and is pretty cool to hang out with. If you're tired of the false religious system, you may want to consider him the Person."

"What if He doesn't speak to me?"

"Trust me, man. Any person who was so desperate to begin a relationship with you that he allowed his only Son to be tortured and die a painful death to bridge some sort of cosmic gap won't play games with your head or give you the silent treatment when you ask him to speak. You just have to earnestly seek him and open your heart."

I smiled at my friend and coughed some more. He laughed at me and took a couple of slow sips of frosty beer. Soon we left the pub. He got hammered that night but not by any type of alcohol. I think he appreciated my painful comments. Somehow he knew that they were different than most and came out of love. I thought about our encounter while walking home. I was thankful. I learned that forced religion sucks, Visine should be carried at all times, and cigars from the Dominican Republic, after a while, taste really good. I also thought about Christianity and how we can sometimes confuse it with a system of following rules and regulations, or even adherence to proper doctrine and theology. True Christianity is first and foremost a relationship with the Living God, and the revelation of proper doctrines and obedience to his commands flows out of that relationship, rather than preceding it.

I played with a man in New York one year who studied films of Nolan Ryan throwing hundred-mile-an-hour fastballs. He also collected his baseball cards, got an autographed jersey at a charity auction, read his biography, and even memorized his stats. However, my teammate never entered into a relationship with the all-time strikeout king because he'd never met him nor did he exchange thoughts and feelings with him. If someone asked him if he knew Nolan Ryan, he would say, "No, I haven't had the chance to meet him yet." If he were ever to meet Nolan and began to converse with him a great deal as he did with his wife, then he could answer that same question by saying, "Yes. As a matter of fact I do. I've not only met him but we talk quite often. I know him extremely well."

I believe that a relationship with God Our Father is the same. We have to spend time with him, too, sharing the same ideas and listening to his replies. It's the same thing we would do with anyone else we hope to know. In fact, there was a religious sect in the Bible who knew more scripture than anyone but when Jesus showed up they wanted nothing to do with him. The very scriptures that pointed to the Messiah they had memorized but kind of missed the whole point of their message.

Ben Ortlip, a friend of mine and fellow author, had an epiphany one time while we were filming a short video for teenagers. Immediately his right hand dove into his blue backpack and came out with a pen. He grabbed some scratch paper and wrote, "Some of our greatest challenges today come from words like Christian, the church, and salvation. These have become synonymous with the subculture known as Christianity. We Christians look a certain way, dress a certain way, talk a certain way, and behave a certain way. We fight against gay rights and abortion. We fight for prayer in school and a voice in our government. We buy out movie theaters to show our solidarity for Christian films. For many of us, these are all part of joining the subculture.

"So instead of Christianity being a simple decision to receive forgiveness for sin and accepting his resurrected life, the notion of coming to Christ has become a lifestyle proposition. Outsiders think coming to Christ means adopting the appearance and practices of the people-group known as Christians. And even though something inside them may be attracted to Jesus and our faith, there's another part that doesn't make any sense to them and drives them away.

"This handed-down lifestyle proposition is a huge obstacle for the gospel. Faith in Christ has been dressed up in the cheap clothes of a subculture called Christianity. More and more, we must undress our spirituality and bring it down to the things that our faith is really all about in the first place, the life and person of Christ, forgiveness, and truth."

Even though it's obvious that Ben is not as good at writing as

Hemingway or even me for that matter, I really liked the points he made. Sometimes we can bring people to the person of Christ and then paint a veil with some lifestyle proposition. Even excellent things like giving, feeding the poor, talking about God, and reading about him won't satisfy us when they are done out of our own resources apart from him or with impure motives.

In retrospect, my time here on this planet has been filled with constant reminders of how the things of this world won't satisfy me. Winning championships and rubbing elbows with famous people like DiMaggio and the president are nice but they won't fill the God-shaped vacuum that Pascal talked about. Not even the subculture of Christianity with all of its nice ten-step marketing schemes promising to give our lives purpose and satisfaction can truly seal my deepest longing for intimate relationship and experience with my God and my Father.

I continue to read my Bible and share with people the unbendable truth that Jesus is the Christ and there is no way to God the Father apart from him but I also talk of receiving that truth, experiencing him, and loving others. For people like me, the ones who recognize his name and hear his voice, only a living vibrant relationship with God will do. I want to live from God and do good things because I love him and have talked to him and want to please him. I want to share about him and inspire others to read the Bible, help people, and feel God's goodness because they love him. I think this desire comes out of me because I have a real relationship with him. And that is what fulfills me on this place we call earth, a relationship with him. Although living in this world and interacting with God can at times be a frustrating battle, I now find the struggle to hear the voice of God and the awe of eternity a beautiful thing. One that I feel is definitely worth my life.

TRYING TO GET LIFE AND ACCEPTANCE FROM THE PAGES OF *PLAYBOY* MAGAZINE

JEFF FOXWORTHY, a redneck comedian, believes that men are simple beings.

Basically, Jeff says, all we want is a beer, and to see something naked. If you give us those two things, then we're happy.

People laughed when he made that comment. But I didn't. I kind of sat there identifying with his statement. *Yes*, I thought to myself. *That's brilliant. Why is that?*

Jeff continued by saying, "You go to a nursing home and see a ninety-year-old man going down the hall using a walker, peeking in rooms. Don't worry. He's not lost. He's probably just finished off a beer in the kitchen and now he's trying to see something naked."

I wish I were more complicated. Maybe even mysterious like Aragorn, the great hidden king in *The Lord of the Rings*, who was first introduced as a woodland ranger as he sat alone in the dark corner of a pub while smoke arose from his pipe. But instead, if I'm honest, there have been many times in this life where I have looked a lot closer to Foxworthy's comical assessment of most men. Only I don't like beer.

I began taking glimpses of naked women while I was very young when an older kid in my neighborhood introduced me to a stash of *Playboy* magazines hidden in the small cubbyhole of a beat-up garage. At first, I could only muster a few peeks in between the pages because I was a little embarrassed at the wonder of a nicely curved female who was mature and without clothing. Somehow I knew that I didn't have the necessary equipment to be with one of them so I looked away rather quickly out of respect for the long wait of growing up that I knew was ahead of me. But after a couple of returns to the garage, I found myself staring longer and longer at the well-fashioned bodies, and those alluring images started to take shape in my memory and travel with me in my subconscious mind often reappearing during the boring moments of my day.

I took a part-time job in fantasyland and began to sit in school daydreaming about being a hero that rescued some damsel in distress imprisoned in a castle that was far, far away. After slaying a scaly green dragon, fighting off a few guards, and taking down some evil dude with a pointed beard like Colonel Sanders, I would run up a long spiral staircase to the top of a white stone tower where one of the models I had recently seen in one of the *Playboy* magazines was waiting for me with no clothes on.

Since I didn't fully understand what the birds and the bees did, we would usually just sit there and look at each other while she sipped tea from a cup and I ate a peanut butter and jelly sandwich. Because I had just rescued her, my eyes freely ran across her naked body without any of the guilt that accompanied me in the garage. She would also smile at me. After I had finished looking her over for about five hours, I would pick up my imaginary centerfold, clothe her with my red silky cape and, amid the cheers, carry her down the steps and lead her out through the village to a distant cottage. It was there that we lived happily ever after and had nine healthy children, a by-product of my continually staring at her with no clothes on. She thanked me for the rest of her days, we never once argued, and I dreamed that my pectorals developed to the point of closely resembling Arnold Schwarzenegger's.

All in all, I thought my fanatisizing would turn out to be pretty harmless. But eventually my hormones arrived, I learned what the bees actually did, and I fell deeper into the hole of dangerous dreaming. I started to experience extreme loneliness as a teenager, feeling disconnected from everyone, which only fueled my desire to see a beautiful girl naked to ease the sorrow of this world. Another well-meaning friend showed me how to rig up the cable television box in my basement so that I could then see in full action what was once limited to mere still photographs. My heart and anything of what was left of my conscience started to harden and watching adult movies became my safe house and refuge for dealing with any sort of real pain and feelings of separation.

I continued down the trail that leads to nowhere during my days of college. After becoming a Christian, my struggles of lust went away for over a year. Like the Bible says, the demons went away for a time to get more invisible friends and came back to visit me with a much stronger army. I started losing the battles of pornography again, which left me wondering if I had really become a Christian at all. That was when I began to say the prayer to receive Christ over and over again, wondering why it wouldn't take. I felt like two different people and both of them felt hypocritical. I kept telling myself that my desire to look at naked women would stop for good when I got married. But it didn't.

I was coming out of a serious relationship when I met my future wife in Baton Rouge, Louisiana. I was looking to train hard and concentrate on baseball so I moved back near my college and lived with a strength trainer for Louisiana State named Terry Grisham. Kymberlee Song-Hee Yip lived next door to me during that fall and we started hanging out as friends. The first time we saw one another she thought I looked a little weird because I have a big forehead and I remember thinking that she had wide nostrils that flared up when she talked. Not exactly the recipe for love at first sight.

The good news for me happened earlier that summer when Kym had gotten into a car accident, which left her scared of driving alone. Somehow, I ended up being put in the passenger seat by my friend Terry as sort of a prank, which I am now very grateful for. She looked a little confused when I walked out to the car that night and the first drive over to the supermarket was rather uncomfortable. Being a small-boned woman, I think she appreciated the fact that I wasn't carrying a roll of gray duct tape or a local map with highlighted directions to the nearest cornfield. At least as far as she knew, anyway. So in the midst of cloudy uneasiness we began to talk on that first fateful drive and we discovered that we were both Christians—serious ones. I really enjoyed her because she was not only pretty but deep words came out of her mouth that were spiritually thick, like *godly* and *holy*. I was reading a book at the time by Jerry Bridges called *The Practice of Godliness*, so I was shocked when the word *godly* leapt off her tongue.

Upon reaching the supermarket, I remember being very drawn to her and thinking how beautiful she was when she reached for a package of sugar high up on one of the shelves. All of a sudden her nostrils looked to be a normal size and I noticed her striking half-Chinese cheekbones that were high up on her face giving her a foreign appeal sort of like a young Meryl Streep. I became aware of the long auburn hair that fell across her shoulders and how it danced halfway down her back. And I loved the shape of her eyes, which sat above those cheekbones. God dipped his brush in tender, deep brown colors when he painted them, and they seemed to talk a language of their own that did not include words.

My thoughts on timing, protocol, and dating changed in a moment, when Wayne said that if I didn't pursue her quickly, someone else would; so I decided to ask her out. I made my move the first chance I got, which happened to be the next day after taking a quick drive down the street together. We were pulling into a parking space at the apartment complex and my nervous foot let up on the clutch before we stopped. I swallowed hard. Since the car was not parked or even in neutral, we shook to a stop. I was embarrassed. I didn't know any skilled pickup lines other than, "Will you go with me?" which I hadn't used since the seventh grade, so naturally my tongue fumbled the ball and I blurted out a question requesting her to hang out with me as more than friends for about two hours a week. It's not real smooth to ask a person to commit to a schedule before you've even been on one date. Stalkers do that sort of thing, not chivalrous men.

Because I looked like a psycho all of a sudden, she very politely said, "No," and camouflaged her answer with some religious Joan of Arc comment about needing her time with God. But by the time we had walked back to her apartment she had changed it to a yes, and the next night we went to a Mexican restaurant called the Superior Grill.

It was the first time she would give me grace for acting like an idiot and the date that followed was something out of the poem "Annabel Lee," one of the greatest romantic appointments that the invisible angels of this world has ever seen. The conversation was so good that I didn't even notice that the World Series was playing in the background and my eyes rarely left hers except to make sure that I was dipping my chips in the salsa cup and not something else. I asked God if that was some sort of sign. He didn't reply.

What I did think was a sign was the fact that my struggle with pornography disappeared while I courted my wife and I rejoiced in the fact that I had found someone who was so amazing I didn't seem to even have a desire to look at anything impure. I didn't undress everyday women on the sidewalks, daydream through boredom, or even feel a pull to glance at the curvy magazine covers that were behind the counters of most convenience stores. Four months later we were engaged and soon after we stood at the altar asking God to be the strength of our union. To this day that request was one of the wisest I have ever made.

It appalled me, however, to find that after a year of marriage to a spectacular godly woman my desire to look at pornography returned. I would go on road trips and still feel the tug to look at unclothed women on television. The times of being away from my wife seemed to re-create those all too familiar feelings of loneliness for me. I started to lose hope and often had slow tears starting to form in the corners of my eyes as I tried to fall asleep.

DARKNESS!

In 1995 I made a trip to Montreal, Canada, to play the Expos. Being the second-largest French-speaking city in the world, I felt like I had actually been planted in Europe, walking around with all kinds of unique shops, restaurants, and people with fancy hats saying *"bonjour"* as I passed them on the beat-up sidewalks. I think the entire city sipped wine, sniffed smelly cheeses, ate caramelized pastries, and smoked fashionable cigarettes in a really cool way as if they had been imitating James Dean in a shiny mirror for years.

Most players on our team didn't mind traveling to the eclectic "City of Mary," which is the original name for Montreal. I was not too fond of it, however, for reasons having nothing to do with hating sugary pastries or anger at secondhand smoke. No. The reason that I hated it so much was for the simple reason that I had a problem focusing on God.

Strip bars littered every other corner and, to my amazement, publicized their establishments by putting life-size posters of fully naked female models right there for all citizens who had healthy eyes to see, children and all. Since I am not blind, the attractive paper advertisements affected my brain.

Most of the nonpostered girls in Ville Marie were beautiful too and all seemed to have that foreign appeal coupled with a sexy accent that could melt an honest man's defenses in no time. I know this because my shield started to melt when I asked one of them for directions to the mall on Ste.-Catherine Street. She told me that I sounded like a cowboy, which really had nothing to do with my question. I scratched my thick beard and left the scene rather quickly.

On my way back to the hotel, I vowed to never ask an attractive girl for directions again unless it was my wife. And for the first time in my life, I totally understood why Billy Graham travels with another man and will not so much as get into an elevator alone with a woman.

I thought back to my days at Churchill Downs and how many of the horses like Justin's Jellybean wore blinders to keep them focused on the race and immune to peripheral distractions such as other horses and fans who were screaming and throwing popcorn. I gently raised my hands and cupped the sides of my fingers so that my eyes could only see the beat-up sidewalk beneath my feet. I began walking back to the hotel, realizing that it was time to stop walking around the city. Occasionally, I widened my hands to make sure that I wasn't going the wrong way but that was about it. I was focused.

When I reached my hotel, Le Centre Sheraton, I breathed a sigh of relief and went up to my room. Upon walking into my finely decorated private quarters, I sat down on the bed and thanked God for keeping my marriage pure and free from the adultery of looking and lusting after fake women on large posters. And real living ones, too. After saying my prayer like it was a lucky charm of protection, I promptly turned on the television and began to peruse the available channels for my viewing entertainment. It was pretty funny to hear Rambo, a tough Green Beret from the eighties, speak in a dubbed French accent. I started laughing. Since the movies on the regular channels weren't doing it for me, I promptly pushed the menu button pretending to myself that I wouldn't be tempted to check out any adult movie since I was feeling spiritually beefy. After all, I had just prayed and I was strong. I wouldn't be ordering one. Therefore, it probably wouldn't even matter if I looked through the Adult Movie Titles to see if they were different from the ones in the United States. I'm not sure why I even needed this information but somehow I felt I did and before I knew it, my right thumb pushed down on the order button that highlighted a French woman in lingerie with a title that eight years of French could not allow me to understand.

One of my favorite things about God is that he never leaves me. He stays with me even when I choose to do or think of something horribly evil. And he sits with me through my poor decisions and hangs around through the pain that occurs afterward. Even if I can't always hear him audibly I respect my Father for sticking it out with me and letting me feel his presence.

Because God is always with me, I remember asking him, "What in the heck am I doing?"

Again, he didn't reply.

"Insanity," Albert Einstein once said, "is doing the same thing over and over again and expecting a different result." And for some stupid reasons that deal with selfishness, loneliness, and male hormones, I seem to make the same decision to look at pictures of naked women over and over again and expect to be fulfilled by them each time I glance, which means either Einstein's definition of the word is wrong or I am insane. Choosing Eve. I keep trying to stuff my inner void with images of different Eves. Why do I think, before I stumble, that God will ease up on the conviction of the Holy Spirit afterward? Do I really think that satisfying my eyes is the answer? Am I really that stupid? Why do I not love God more with my actions and respect my wife as the precious gift that she is? It doesn't make sense to me. My wife and I have a great sexual relationship, which only serves to confuse me even further.

Maybe it has nothing to do with her and lingers more in the area of my selfishness and improper feelings of entitlement.

It has also been very hard for me to apologize to God when I do the same thing over and over. If I tell him, "I was wrong a few moments ago. I am sorry. Thank you for your forgiveness—again," I feel like a broken record or some worn-out skipping disco record from the seventies that is very tired and beat up. I feel like I am scratched and don't really mean what I say. My emotions tell me that I'm faking it. "I am a big fat liar," they whisper. "If I were really sorry, I would cut out the garbage, entirely."

It is written that if a righteous man falls seven times, he picks himself up seven times (Proverbs 24:16, my paraphrase). I loved that verse until I fell a few times past seven. What if you have fallen seventy-seven times? Is there a point where rising up from the mat becomes ridiculous and you stay down for the ten count? I hope not.

The Apostle Paul penned some of the most fabulous sentences ever constructed when he wrote in the seventh chapter of Romans, "I do not understand what I do. When I want to do good, evil is right there with me hanging on me like a dead corpse weighing me down. I want to do what is good and right but I can't seem to carry it out. For in my inner being, I delight in God's Law; but I see another law that is at work among the members of my body. It wages war against my body and makes my flesh a sinful prisoner. What a miserable man that I am! Who will rescue me from this body of death?" (verses 15–24, my paraphrase).

I am so overwhelmed that the man who inspirationally wrote most of the New Testament is so honest with his pen by admitting the fact that sin still entangled him as he walked on this planet. Sincerity of heart mixed with courage has always been very beautiful to me and I needed this verse to gnaw on over the years like a dog that takes his time with a meaty bone under some distant shade tree. It has encouraged me and on many an occasion God has used the Great Apostle Paul's words to keep me from throwing in the towel.

Paul answers his own question of who will be doing the rescuing in the next sentence when he says, "Praise be to God through Jesus Christ Our Lord! He will rescue me! For on one hand I serve the law of God with my mind but flesh seems to serve the law of sin" (Romans 7:25, my paraphrase).

Sometimes I get angry and want to beat my body and make it my slave.

Pornography is a word that originates and bathes in the definition of being anything that is visually designed to stimulate a person sexually. By its original definition even some of our most popular billboards involving owls and attractive women showing cleavage would fit the bill. I guess this disqualifies the old J.C. Penney catalogs that featured women in underwear since the ads were designed to sell brassieres.

My friend Ben Ortlip explained to me one day that when a person has sex or becomes stimulated sexually, the brain releases dopamine, which is a feel-good chemical that oozes over our synapses, giving us a rush. Each country has its problems but he believes that our technological advances with medialike computers and satellite television have made pornography America's unspoken epidemic. It's an epidemic that we don't talk about even though it is now quietly available in almost every suburban home. I think Ben is right.

Like so many people, I get the urge to justify my lustful behavior by twisting scripture or the law on my heart that gives me no peace when I am looking at things I shouldn't be viewing. Instead of just admitting that something is not of God and I struggle with it, I feel the temptation to explain it away with trickery. I hear silent voices inside my head that say, "At least you're not out like some of the other guys who are running the town," or, "This is totally natural for someone like you, a guy with testosterone." I keep having to tell them to "Shut up!"

Some people think that marital infidelity is not wrong. I had a player tell me one time that there was no such thing as a married man one hundred miles away from home. I thought that was sad. I was glad I never had to look his wife in the eye. Another time I had a Christian friend tell me that he started to cheat on his wife because she had stopped "giving it up" at home. I thought that was sad too. I counseled him. He didn't tell his sneaky voice to shut up.

"Harmless fantasy," a famous radio DJ once said about pornography. But the truth is it assists in tearing up our lives and our families through chemical alteration of our brains and physical covetousness.

In a chilling scene from the movie *The Silence of the Lambs*, Clarice Starling, a young detective, quizzes a brilliant psychotic killer named Dr. Hannibal Lecter as he sits behind bars. She is hoping to get inside his mind to increase her chances of catching another serial killer, Buffalo Bill, who was currently at large. She had sent him the case files to go over. Instead of answering Clarice's questions, he tells her everything she needs to find Buffalo Bill is in those files.

She peers through the vertical iron poles with her face only a few feet away and in desperation asks how.

"First principles, Clarice. Simplicity. Read Marcus Aurelius.

Of each particular thing ask: What is it in itself? What is its nature . . . ?"

Dr. Lecter then asks what Buffalo Bill does.

Clarice begins to answer, only to be cut off almost immediately.

"No! What is the principle thing Buffalo Bill does? And what need does it serve?"

Clarice again begins to answer, only to be cut off again.

"No! He covets. That's his nature. And how do we begin to covet, Clarice? Do we seek out things to covet? Make an effort to answer now."

"No, we just . . ."

Again Dr. Lecter interrupts her and the man who is deemed to be clinically insane delivers a powerful answer to his own question.

"No . . . we begin by coveting what we see every day."

Conquest of the eyes.

And that is the danger of pornography, sexual sin, and the things we allow our eyes to see on a daily basis. It causes us to covet. Although it is no longer the Christian's inner nature to covet, I wish I could say the same for our flesh. Pictures feed our soft tissue and cause our bodies to enter into addiction and covetousness. And when we focus our eyes and hearts on the creation rather than Our Creator, our desires begin to wander. It is like a drug that numbs our hearts to God and the value that he has put on women and their bodies. It is a bribe that corrupts our treasured women and thoughts. We begin to need more and more pictures and in a different variety. We start to look and undress everyday women that walk across the street and our minds run wild in the land of imagination.

Eventually that covetousness grows past the fake posters and into the lives and bedrooms of the living. Our view of what is right and proper becomes perverted. And when that happens families begin to separate and the children of men begin to live in despair, growing up with fathers who are focused on the wrong thing or not even there at all. Sadly, many couples end up divorced, not even knowing about one of the arrows that hit them until it is too late. It seems that the sins of fathers really are handed down to the generations that follow. If we don't pay attention, the cycles of sexual obsession or abuse almost always will continue.

The problem that I have is not actually our struggles with sexual sin, but that almost all the men I know don't even seem to care. If a man broke into your house to rape your wife, I think it safe to say that any man worth his salt would fight the intruder to the bitter end. But when pornography introduces itself over the television set or computer we welcome it. The country welcomes it. We make no connection that this is a media proved to damage marriages, weaken households, and elevate sexual sin in a nation.

It's as if we stand around dazed and confused, saying, "Some doctors recommend it, so I think it's okay."

We get disgusted at the pedophile but allow him suitable avenues to prowl. And as a nation, we cry at the Jim Jones tragedy saying to ourselves, "How could people be so stupid and gullible?" as we chug down Satan's own version of Kool-Aid for ourselves.

I know because I have sipped the polluted juice myself.

I read an article recently by Shelley Lubben, a former porn star who had given her life to Jesus Christ. She said, "Most women who turn to porn acting as a money-making enterprise didn't grow up in a healthy childhood . . . Indeed, many actresses admit they've experienced sexual abuse, physical abuse, verbal abuse and neglect by parents. Some were raped by relatives and molested by neighbors . . . So we were taught at a young age that sex made us valuable. The same horrible violations we experienced then, we relive as we perform our tricks for you in front of the camera. And we hate every minute of it. We're traumatized little girls living on anti-depressants, drugs and alcohol acting out our pain in front of you who continue to abuse us."[1]

Shelley continued the article by taking responsibility for her own actions, by admitting a lust for power and money, but I could not get past my participation in her emotional pain by being an addicted consumer.

I learned from her website that the largest group of Internet pornography viewers are young adults between the ages of twelve and seventeen. I also thought it was really sad when she said that many women hate being degraded by foul-smelling men so badly that they throw up in between scenes or chain-smoke cigarettes to calm themselves down. That's a far cry from their provocative eyes, which seem to say, "I want you. Really bad!"

The first time I confessed to my wife that my struggle with pornography had come back was after that previously mentioned, ill-fated trip to Montreal, Canada. I use the words "come back," because for a long time after meeting my wife the desire to look at naked women had gone away.

I would like to think that I was responsible for having the courage to be honest with her but it really didn't happen that way. The truth is, we were going to be together physically and before kissing her, I became very emotional and started to cry. I couldn't be with her after a road trip of complete collapses with hotel room movies and adult previews in a foreign land. In my heart, I felt like such a fake. Minutes before, when I looked in a mirror, I imagined myself to be some scam artist with bad hair that prostitutes Jesus on television and has ulterior motives like money and fame. Now, I was going to pretend that I was genuine and take advantage of my beautiful bride who was waiting for her knight in shining armor to return. I hurt. I wanted to be different.

When my wife asked me what was wrong, I told her in the best way that I knew how what had been going on with me.

"I have been struggling with pornography again," I said to her with a choking voice wondering if she might hate me, not talk to me for days or even worse, leave me. My heart skipped in fear.

"How long has this been going on?"

"Months," I replied.

"Why didn't you tell me?"

"I have been way too embarrassed. I mean, here I have you and I love you so much. Your body is awesome. And then days later, I'm looking at some naked woman's body on television who I really don't care anything about. I feel like a drug addict that can't stop himself. Like I go on cruise control or something. I'm trying to fight this. I read the Bible and pray and ask God to take the desire away but it doesn't seem to happen. I feel like a fake. I am so sorry."

My wife responded with a smile. One that said, I love you. And even though she too had watery emotions that were spilling out of her, they were ones of acceptance and not condemnation, which sort of confused me.

"Thank you for telling me this," she said with a gentle voice.

"Thank you? You mean you're not mad at me and you're not going to leave me?"

"I don't like what you have been doing but I still love you. And leave you? No. Why would I do that? You're my husband."

"I might be your husband but let's face it, when you married me you got damaged goods. I came into this relationship with a lot of baggage. And now you're carrying it. I'm so sorry. I thought my fight against pornography had stopped for good when I met you."

Again my wife smiled. "When I married you I didn't get damaged goods. I got a godly man."

"How can you say that?" I asked in frustration, needing and almost wanting some type of verbal punishment.

"I can say that because a godly man is not a person that doesn't have struggles. A godly man is a person who fights against sin and is honest with his wife. He tells her the truth. And that is what you've done."

More tears slowly began to spill out from the corners of my eyes as once again, I was being ministered to by that same word, *godly*. I felt like a grown-up Humpty Dumpty that was being put back together again with the superglue of kind words, forgiveness, and acceptance.

I knew that the love of God broke out of us that night and had some sort of intervention with me. I had wanted to keep things hidden and private. Because sin manifests itself and grows stronger in dark and secret places, I really believe that I would have been in trouble if the Holy Spirit hadn't taken over in that situation. Asking God to become our strength at the altar on Canal Street was very wise. He came through. God is so good but his goodness always comes out in ways that are not familiar to me and when I least expect it. Sometimes it's painful. And I sure wasn't ready for the acceptance and love that overflowed from my wife. I felt like a person who somehow really did love and belong to God after all, even though my behavior was poor. It was freeing.

If we let him, he uses the sins of man and the pain of this world to mold us into men who walk along the bridge of life somehow limping with honor.

We looked each other in the eyes really deeply that night and we made love in a manner more passionate than we ever had before. We had a connection that was in our souls. A link that was more than just two bodies coming together as one. I learned about true marital intimacy and I experienced it in different ways than I ever had before. On all levels. Although I can't write too much more about the event without sounding like *Mutual of Omaha's Wild Kingdom* narrator or a cheesy romance novelist, I will tell you that we conceived our first child that night. It was a gift I did not deserve. But then again God doesn't really owe me anything. He's just good at giving.

I would like to tell you that I no longer struggle with this issue and permanent healing took place within me when my wife extended forgiveness after that trip to Montreal, but I can't. Life on the road in Major League Baseball has been for the most part a very lonely time for me, which exposes this desire to see something naked and feel accepted, regardless of the town. It's not baseball's fault; it's mine. I made poor choices as a young adolescent boy growing up and chose to fill emotional voids with alluring images. I didn't know that this pattern of inoculating myself with a dose of counterfeit acceptance from magazines and the television set would follow me into adulthood but it has.

Henri Nouwen, in his book *The Only Necessary Thing*, said that loneliness is one of the greatest sources of suffering today. He called it "the disease of our lifetime." I've found Henri's statement to be very accurate. I am amazed that this generation, which has developed the best methods for communication, is the loneliest.

Some therapists and sociologists say that many addictions are generational. And most sexual addicts suffer from intense feelings of loneliness and don't even know it. I think that is why most men fantasize about being accepted, being wanted, and having someone that wishes to be close to them. I have never heard of a pornography film where the woman walks away after being propositioned, leaving the man sitting there alone. It just doesn't happen. And if it was about the orgasm for a man we could just look at a wall and take care of it but we don't. We need the fantasy of approval and we want to imagine that someone desires us, too. In our minds we drift off and open the door to a world that eventually desensitizes our hearts.

A friend of mine named John Rivenbark says that many times we are looking for qualities in others that we do not see in ourselves. When we are young, we are attracted to older women who make us feel manly and that we have what it takes. If an older woman acts as if she was interested in us, we get excited immediately. And when we grow up and get a few wrinkles, younger women appeal to us for a different reason, as if a pretty young woman could give us the feeling that we aren't so old and we've still got it.

I also know Christian men who struggle with varying degrees of same-sex attraction and homosexual urges. They are not necessarily gay. They are just people that have trusted in Jesus to be their life but struggle with the need to be held by other men. One of them confessed to me recently that he desires to be with men who look very masculine. He told me that as a young boy he felt very emasculated because he wasn't good at sports. Athletic bloodlines ran in his family and his father was considered one of the best coaches in town. Because his father died while my friend was still a boy, he was never held, wrestled with, or even given a hug by an older man or father figure. No one stepped up and took an interest in him. He felt abandoned by males! When he got older and found himself attracted to other men, a lot of times the meetings with men were not about the sexual contact. They were about being held by a stronger, and in his eyes, a more masculine man who would affirm him by telling him that he was okay. He said that he actually felt more of a man when he left the hotel room after being with a man, than the times he spent with a woman.

I believe the problem or void within us goes even deeper than our sexual behavior, straight acting or not. For some reason, a lot of us attempt to find personal and spiritual validation through sexual exploits. For the majority of us, those trips are heterosexual, but for reasons that I don't understand, some of those trips are same-sex oriented. But all of us ache to feel manly and to believe we are accepted by God for who we are. Only Jesus in his infinite wisdom knows what our struggles are really all about. But I further believe that whatever shape the sexual dysfunction takes, Jesus not only understands it, he also cares about it and longs to heal us and set us free from our addiction to counterfeit life. He wants to reach deep within the core of our being and fill the emptiness with himself.

John Eldredge, the author of *Wild at Heart*, said that true worship is that which you give your heart to, expecting life in return.

Although I have given my heart to God and he has it safe, I am tired of sitting in worship services that focused on the Creation rather than the Creator who is soon to be forever praised. Amen! Again, worshipping the creation is, in part, what pornography is all about. Somehow I've come to believe that those naked images can give me life. I'm just trying to figure out why I continue to focus on those idols, even after knowing the pictures are nothing but a dead end and knowing that God loves me in heaping amounts. For some reason, I keep stepping on stupid.

A really pivotal moment in my relationship with God came during one of those disgusting worship services I didn't really want to be a part of but somehow ended up participating in. I was watching an adult movie clip over the Internet and once again asking God why I continued to view obscene material.

"Why am I doing this?"

I have yet to hear God answer me audibly or with a thunderous voice like he did some people in the Bible. A lot of times, I hear crickets, which are the same little chirping insects that sound off when Daffy Duck introduces himself. But this time I did not. I can't explain how, but I heard him in my own voice as if there were two of me but I knew that it wasn't really me talking.

God replied.

What I learned from God is that I was more focused and concerned with my struggle of sexual sin than I was with him. Once again, as I seem to say somewhere in each chapter of this book, I cried. Winning and losing in my own battle of sexual sin had somehow become the focus of my relationship with God and not the relationship itself. I had gotten off-track and became involved in a sin-management program with occasional redundant prayer, which has absolutely nothing to do with the gospel. I felt good about myself when I had gone long periods of time without falling and when I went through a binge in some far-away hotel, I felt spiritually crummy. My walk and relationship with God were based on how successful I was with not looking at pornography, especially on major league road trips. It was all wrapped up in the amount of my sin, which I now see as being very sad. I turned off the computer, fell to my knees, and began talking to God. I was thankful that my Father had shown up and pulled me out of a technological strip bar. I got up without saying amen knowing that I would never be signing off. I rejoiced. God always has my back.

After that time, I have done much better with my eyes. I think it is mainly because I am more focused on God than my struggle. I still care if I stumble but conquering pornography is no longer the "end all and be all" of my Christian walk. Jesus is.

And that is a beautiful thing!

Years after my revelation, Kym and I vacationed at the Jalousie Plantation in St. Lucia. We stayed in a villa that was right between the Grand Pitons, which are two ginormous mountains on the southwest part of the island. My wife and I were there for our thirteenth wedding anniversary. We usually drive an hour or so away from our home to the north Georgia mountains for a romantic weekend. This time, for some unknown reason, we decided to do things a little differently and step it up.

There is something magical about the Val des Pitons. Oprah Winfrey says it's one of the five places that you must visit in your lifetime. The sun melts between them over the water at the end of the day, perfectly casting a soft glow that rises up each mountain's edge until blackness takes over. That's when the stars come out and shine their wonder. Because there is little human light from the villas on the hillside, I feel like I am in a planetarium on some grade school field trip seeing constellations that I would otherwise never see. Although I don't know their names, I appreciate the fact that God does and the fact that he has hung all of them in splendor as if this world is a crib and we are his children who need to be entertained by a shiny heavenly mobile.

One afternoon, long before sunset, there was a girl sitting next to us on the beach who was from England. My wife and I loved her accent as she talked to her boyfriend with thick British tones and used words that I had heard only in movies. I felt the urge to imitate the couple's accent, so I tried my best British accent.

Kym shushed me by saying, "Stop that, they'll hear you. You're going to embarrass me on our first day here."

I quit, but after some light interrogation Kym admitted that my accent came across rather well. She likened me to a young James Bond. I liked that. I kept waiting for a waiter on the beach to come up and tell me I had a special assignment from Q or something, but it never happened.

Anyway, as my beautiful bride and I were sitting there playing cards together, I couldn't help noticing out of the corner of my eye that the British girl on the beach had taken her top off.

In that moment, I thought of my wife who didn't know my eyes were checking out this shapely young woman. I thought of my dark brown, nontransparent sunglasses. I felt bad. I remembered Foxworthy's statement, and I thought of how I related to him suggesting that men of all ages are quite simple beings really and only want an enjoyable drink and to see something naked. Again, shallowness.

I was disappointed that I wasn't more complicated and yet I also felt good about knowing that I wasn't alone in all of this and that there were other men that fall to temptation and let their eyes wallow in muddy piglike slop. I thought about God and focusing on him. I looked back at my wife under my suspicious glasses without her even knowing it.

I leaned over to Kym and whispered, "The British girl has taken her top off and I can't stop looking."

"Wow, I hope this is a topless beach," she replied. "She can get in trouble for that."

"Did you even hear me?"

"Yes."

"I'm confessing to you."

"I know. So get over it," she said. "Start focusing on me."

"Thanks," I replied back, in a much more relaxed voice but still at a whisper. "I needed that! I'm going to be staring at you for a while, so don't get upset if I appear fixated. Okay?"

"That's what I'm here for," she said back with a smile.

Since we had been in the shade all along, I lifted my sunglasses and rested them on the top of my head. I thought of the Old Testament verse that says: "May you rejoice in the wife of your youth and may her breasts satisfy you always." At that point, I was. And they have. I was honoring and focusing on God by living in the present and looking at my wife whom he asks me to love as Jesus loves us, his Church of people.

That was such great advice from Kym. Most of my problems in life have to do with not focusing on God and the gifts he has given me. It is not just limited to pornography. I seem to be a lot like the apostle in the boat who hops up and looks at crashing waves, instead of focusing upon Jesus, who is standing out on the water doing something miraculous. When that happens, I always start to sink. I think of myself and what I am doing, whether good or bad, and take a dive. Although my life is in Christ, my mind has to continually remind my eyes to focus on that which is unseen or notice him in the things that are, like my wife. So the bigger picture for me now is how to honor my heavenly Father and walk upright in a place where worldly problems and pictures try to tear me down.

I have victory today over pornography not because I don't at times struggle with temptation and even occasionally yield to it but for the reason that I am no longer mastered by it. Conquering sexual sin is no longer the focus of my walk, God is. Because sin is no longer my authority figure, I have learned to refocus on him when I fall and by his strength, pick myself up.

Eventually, the temptations of this world will loosen their grip on our lives when we look to God. I don't know if the Devil truly flees or we just become so caught up in the personhood of God that we no longer notice the evil delights that sit on the table next to us. Regardless, the victory is not won by following a twelve-step process or going through some self-help group that teaches us to clean up our lives apart from him. It is won by Christ, his life, looking at and receiving him. Period!

As I dealt another card to my wife knowing that I was going to win yet another game of gin, I thought of the supernatural power of God and how he is available for the single, the married, and the hurting people throughout the world. I thought of his availability to people in all walks of life at the same time and how he is there regardless of the different struggles that each might endure. I thought of the single mom, the abandoned child, the movie star, and the man who is trying to run the crowded drive thru at Chick-fil-A. I smiled.

My thoughts reminded me of David when he said, "Even the darkness will not be dark to you!" (Psalm 139:12 NIV).

I thanked God for being available to us at all times and in all circumstances. After all, we are constantly connected to him for our viewing and talking pleasure, whether in a quiet and dark hotel room or on a beautiful, bright, and sunny beach.

5

AMAZING GRAYSON!

IN *THE RAGAMUFFIN GOSPEL*, Brennan Manning writes, "For Grace proclaims the awesome truth that all is a gift. All that is good is ours not by right but by the sheer bounty of a gracious God. While there is much we may have earned—our degree and our salary, our home and garden, a Miller Lite and a good night's sleep—all this is possible only because we have been given so much."[1]

Even though I don't care for frosty beers, I really liked Brennan's statement into the sheer bounty of a gracious God. It hit me hard.

Another time of deep emotion came while watching *Les Misérables*. The opening scene of that movie was so grace-giving that it moved me to tears. Liam Neeson played a traveling convict named Jean Valjean who had just finished serving twenty years hard labor for stealing a loaf of bread. After sleeping a while on a hard wooden bench, an older lady pokes him and insists that he ask to stay the night at an inn that belonged to a bishop. Even though the bishop gave him a meal and a bed to rest his tired body in, Valjean got up in the middle of the night, punched the bishop in the face, and stole what he thought was all of the holy man's expensive silverware.

The next day the French police caught Valjean and brought him back to the bishop. Because I knew absolutely nothing about the story, I was excited to see that the authorities had caught Valjean and the bishop was going to get back his silverware, the only things he seemed to physically possess that had any worldly value. But to my amazement and the shock of most everyone else in the theater, the silver-haired bishop told the police that he intentionally gave Valjean the silverware. The bishop continued to confuse me when he said, "But I told him to take the candlesticks too and I noticed he forgot them. Go and fetch the candlesticks!"

And with that, a woman named Madame Gilot raced off to get the prized silver and shiny candlesticks. As I sat dumbfounded in my chair in the theater, Valjean stood up on the big screen looking equally astonished and suspicious of a punishment that he somehow escaped.

After filling up the convict's bag with more costly silver, the bishop pulled off a dirty brown hood that covered the head of the shamed thief and said, "Jean Valjean, my brother, you no longer belong to evil. With this silver, I bought your soul. I've ransomed you from fear and hatred. And now I give you back to God."

It worked. Jean Valjean became a new man, turned his life around, and continued to extend grace to others the rest of the movie. I was pretty much awestruck!

I have found at times that playing Major League Baseball and living in America is not exactly the best recipe for someone like me who wants to walk with God. Like the criminal in *Les Misérables*, I keep getting presented with options to get my needs met from something or someone other than God. My temptations have not just been limited to improper sexual thoughts, either. I have felt a strong desire to cheat and make more money by scuffing baseballs and spitting on them or cheat the government by telling them that my home is in Florida instead of Georgia so that I wouldn't have to pay any state income tax. There was also a time in baseball when I took a prescribed hormone and felt the urge to increase my dose wondering if it would make my slow fastball cross home plate with a lot more speed. And in the late nineties, when I started to make a lot of money, I felt the enticement to let my bank account become my life source and safety net instead of God. Small amounts of fame have been addicting for me, too, and I have wrestled with the temptation to think that I am somehow better than other men simply because certain people have wanted my autograph.

DISGUSTING!

I also know that these temptations are not exclusive to me or other pro athletes. I know that many people of all ages and walks of life have had similar struggles that probably show up in different forms and desires regardless of how much money they have or what season of life they are currently encountering. I suppose that almost all temptations for the Christian basically come down to the same thing, the lure to walk and become satisfied independently from God.

Even though we may have some horribly disgusting thoughts or temptations that dance across our brains, we have not sinned simply because the enemies of this world have presented us with options for living other than God. In fact, I don't even believe that temptation is a bad thing. I mean how could we fully express our love for God if we weren't tempted to make Jesus get out of the driver's seat of our lives and occasionally ride shotgun? I'm also tempted to think that it's in these crashing moments when we do steer our lives independently from God, that we need to know about God's grace.

I've found that in this life it's so easy for me to get excited about grace, even talk about it and learn various definitions for it or sit in a church service that follows with the singing of John Newton's classic hymn "Amazing Grace." The problem comes when someone offends me or some crazy fan that probably needs to be on a calming medication sits behind my wife at a ball game and says something derogatory to her about me while saliva starts to drip from the corners of his mouth. Or the time when I got scammed in Puerto Rico by lending my landlord money only to see her disappear. I have trouble giving grace and forgiving when it hurts the most. It seems to me that I only want to dish out grace for the petty sins like picking your nose in public or gossiping at the local sandwich shop. It's in these moments that I pray to be reminded of the forgiveness and grace that have already been extended to me. If I forget these times, I will never be able to hand it out to someone else.

After playing my first year in the big leagues with the amazin' New York Mets, Kym and I lived with my brother Rick for a couple of weeks. During that time, Kym walked into the first-floor bathroom and took a pregnancy test. A blue line appeared between the plastic sides and we discovered that she was carrying another person in her body. It was a very powerful moment for the both of us. I didn't cry. I just stared at a tall framed poster of Bryce Canyon that hung against my brother's wall with my chin on my hand like the famous statue of *The Thinker*. I was frozen. I wasn't upset. I just sat and basked in the numbing amazement that I was a father.

When Kym walked out of the bathroom, I asked her if I could help but she said that I had done quite enough already. She smiled. I looked at her belly. I smiled.

I could hardly believe that a little boy or girl was growing inside of her. We were very happy and yet terrified at the same time. You don't need a degree or special training to become a father, only working body parts, a good adoption lawyer, or a doctor who is skilled in the art of test tubes.

There have been times in my life where my emotions have moved past any form of tears or emotional high fives and I have found myself simply frozen. Like the time I helped lead a retreat at St. Xavier and after talking about God in small groups, we all watched Mookie Wilson's ground ball roll through Bill Buckner's legs to tie game six of the 1986 World Series. I just sat there thinking, "Did that really just happen?" I had that same sort of feeling in my gut when my wife announced to me that she was pregnant. I was excited at being a father, but I couldn't help sitting in confusion as well. I knew our only time of unprotected sex happened to be the night of my confession after returning from Montreal. The night she received my embarrassing nakedness. And a child was born out of it. I didn't understand why God would allow something good to happen to me when I had fallen so short in honoring him. As it says in Isaiah, I guess God really does give beauty for ashes.

Kym and I soon purchased a book called *What to Expect When You're Expecting*, which is sort of a childbirth manual for dummies. We read some pages together and I found out that embryos of men really are different than that of a monkey. I looked at a child's developmental timeline and learned that from a very early age in the womb children have a brain and can actually hear and process sounds from our world, which fascinated me.

Months later, about the time of fetal hearing, I remember looking at my wife while we were staying with her grandparents in the upstairs bedroom of their Chinese home in Metairie, Louisiana. She was about six months pregnant and trying to fall asleep. I looked at her little volleyball-sized stomach sticking out from the middle of her body as she lay there on her back. I guess being pregnant feels like another person is relentlessly hanging onto you while never giving you a break. She looked like a person trying to make a snow angel as she waved her arms back and forth moving the bed covers off her overheated body. Eventually, most of the covers ended up on the floor. She was miserable.

Earlier in the day, as we walked through a mall, Kym had burst into tears when I didn't want to try a piece of chocolate fudge that she bought from a candy store. I wasn't being a poor sport; I was in training and I knew that if I had a smidgen, I would scarf down the entire slice and go to the store for more. Knowing my limitations as a recovering sugar addict, I refused. But to her biological female chemicals, that was totally unacceptable and downright mean. She had a complete breakdown on one of the benches in the middle of that mall as older ladies walked past me with looks that sneered. They didn't speak, but used their eyes as weapons that daggered out the words, "You jerk!"

I felt horrible. I knew I should have tried the fudge. What an idiot!

So in an effort to please the little old sometimes-nice ladies and live with my wife in peace, I broke a small corner of good-tasting chocolate fat off the fudge bar that I pulled out from the brown bag. I made eye contact with Kym and ate the piece of fudge with a sheepish grin.

"Mmm," I said. "This tastes great."

"Are you mocking me?" she asked. "I want you to know that I am totally disgusted with you right now. As soon as I can get control of myself, we are leaving!"

I didn't respond. I just sat there thinking to myself, *Who is this new person that I am married to?*

HORMONES!

So that night as she lay in the bed, huffing and puffing, frustrated over her uncomfortable pregnancy, I remembered life on that bench in the mall and thought about asking aloud in the darkness, "Need some fudge?" But I didn't. I actually had the good sense to realize that I really would have been mocking her at that point. And somehow, I didn't remember nighttime ridicule as being one of her many more than five "love languages."

Because I am fond of Downy-smelling covers, I just quietly moved to the ground among discarded blankets like a man taking cover behind sandbags in a well-barricaded foxhole. After a time, light skipped through the panes of glass from the other side of the room making a round shadow of her dome-shaped stomach on the wall. I kept staring at the moon and decided to have some fun with its shimmering tone. I made various animal figures with my hands in the moonlight that danced on top of the shadow of her stomach. Eventually the rabbits hopping over the big round hill got on her nerves and I was forced to quit the puppet show early and lie still on my back not saying a word.

After more time had passed, I hurt for her tiny whimpers and got serious. I asked if we could pray together. After kneeling over the side of the bed while clutching her round belly and saying a few words aimed at God, I started to talk to our child. Because we declined to know the sex of our child, I felt a little awkward not knowing how to address our unborn baby. I started by saying, "Hey, you, when are you going to come see me?" I put my ear to her stomach. I didn't hear anything. I continued to speak, "We love you so much. Your mom and I can't wait to hold you."

I spoke to our son, having never seen his face and without even knowing that he was a boy. I approached him in a way that was extremely intimate. Even though I had never personally interacted with him, I loved him with a greater passion than I loved my own self. It was a very moving experience.

Right there, kneeling on the ground, God began to teach me. I realized I was acting somewhat like God the Father. I saw that my wife housed another person inside herself just as Jesus shelters us, the body of Christ. I was connected to and dependent on Jesus, just as my unborn child was dependent on Kym. And even though God's voice may be at times a little muffled, I do hear my heavenly Father talk to me. I fight to get clarity here on earth but ultimately I know a time is coming when I will leave this world and experience a complete birth into a new realm called heaven. Sometime soon my heavenly Father will deliver me and hold me while looking in my eyes; even now the scriptures tell me that my Lord shields me and cares for me, while guarding me as the apple of his eye.

I also continued to be reminded of the grace that my wife gave me after returning from Canada as I knelt over my child in the womb. Once again I was reminded about the gentle hand of

God through the forgiveness of my wife. I was quiet and I was thankful.

I used to tease my wife asking her what we were going to do if we had a boy who had her soft Asianlike eyes and red hair. She gave an emphatic, "Stop it! He might hear you!" Even though I secretly feared having a girl with my forehead, I was very excited about seeing our child for the first time. It somewhat consumed me.

When my son was delivered, true to form, he had red hair and my wife's eyes. I had never seen a red-haired Chinese boy before but he was unusually striking in a good way. After the doctor suctioned out his throat with an extra-large plastic tool, something looking like an eyedropper, my son began to scream. He was uncomfortable in his new world. Because he was big, the nurses put him under a heat lamp in a glass crib and walked away. He looked like a turtle, overturned on his back, wiggling his arms and legs. He kept crying very hard.

I walked over to him and let him grab my pinkie, saying softly, "Hey, buddy. I knew you were going to come out and see me."

Our eyes met each other for the first time. And my son was still. He squeezed my hand very hard and stopped crying.

The doctor asked me, "Have you been talking to him?"

"Yes."

"I can tell. He knows your voice."

"Really?" I questioned.

"I always know the fathers who talk to their children. Most of the time their kids get quiet right away and listen to them. Your voice is the only thing familiar to him right now. He's not even used to freely moving his arms and legs."

My son and I continued to look each other in the eye and I kept calming him down with my voice. I had no idea if he could focus on my face but my eyes worked just fine and I couldn't stop looking him over as I spoke.

"You need to step away from him now and be quiet," the doctor said. "He needs to cry. He needs to get out any leftover mucus that might be in his lungs."

I stepped back and was silent. He screamed as loud as he could when I pulled my little finger from his grasp. The sounds of my son's cries were sweet nectar to my ears and more powerful than a popular church hymn that has survived centuries of changing cultures. I wept. I stuck out my arm and blessed him. I told my son his name. It was Grayson. We named him Grayson after a nickname that my father used to call me as a child. A teammate asked me a few years later if we named him that because of the biblical word *grace*. Although that purposeful designation had never come to my mind, he truly was a gift and one born from the grace of God and forgiveness of my wife. He was the grace son. He was Amazing Grayson!

Over many days, I couldn't stop looking at Grayson. Even asleep, I appreciated his rhythmic breathing. I would sneak into his dimly lit bedroom watching the covers slightly rise and fall. When I looked at him, I had trouble understanding why God allowed Kym to become pregnant after I had failed miserably with my eyes while hanging out in Montreal. It still didn't make any sense to me. No reporter had ever written something nice about me after I had pitched poorly. And growing up, I'd gotten pats on the back for showing my parents good report cards, not bad ones.

Grayson is but one of the many evidences of God's mercy and grace that has been extended to me over the years. And the truth is I will always need his grace. The Bible says that it is God's kindness that leads a person to repentance and it is his grace that enables us to walk in him. For the first time in my life, I really understood that God actually liked me and looked upon me with great care similar to the way I looked at Grayson as he just sat there and slept. Before my first son was born, I really think I performed too much for God instead of living from his acceptance as a child. I also believe I shared Jesus with people hoping that God would like me better if I convinced more people to believe in his Son. As if I could even do that in the first place. But after experiencing Amazing Grayson, I learned to rest in the fact that God was pleased with the deepest part of me even if he didn't like some of my outward behavior. And that understanding motivated me to change my behavior. I mean if God loved me enough to allow his only Son to be tortured and killed to repair a relationship with me when I wanted nothing to do with him, I wondered how much he cared for me after I had apologized and made amends.

After Grayson's arrival, when someone asked me about Jesus, I began to talk about the fatherhood of God and his great love for each and every one of us. I stopped selling Jesus like that new stereo at Circuit City and I quit talking about the better lifestyle that Jesus offered and eternal happiness brought about by escaping flames. In short, I stopped making the gospel about something God could offer us other than his Son and I began to talk about his great love for us, demonstrated by his grace, which is a lot more attractive than the religious efforts of mankind.

GRACE!

I'm sure some people might try to find an illusionary loophole in God's economy and use grace as a license to sin or do whatever they want. I know that I drifted in and out of that kind of thinking back in my early days of considering Jesus. I used to get angry at a rebuke, even monitoring its possibly preachy delivery or trying to be a lawyer instead of receiving it with humility. I have also felt the temptation to use grace and justify poor behavior that deep down inside I know is wrong but can't seem to master. At times, even now, I want to dismiss some of my poor behavior as being perfectly normal or I attempt to justify it by saying that it's part of this difficult life we live here on a fallen earth. I am ashamed to admit that on more than one occasion, I have tried to stuff down the unpleasantness of conviction and cut a deal to struggle with small sins instead of major ones, like looking instead of touching, or thinking instead of doing. I know that I am no longer condemned in the eyes of God but I am so thankful that he doesn't allow me to get away with this kind of attitude and quickly cracks my slowly hardening heart with a gentle conviction, bringing me back to the battle of loving and following him without compromise. He will not let me use his grace as a license to sin. He loves me too much. And I am thankful for that. I don't want to spend God's kindness without care.

One of my favorite biblical writers said, "For the grace of God has appeared, bringing salvation to all people. It trains us to reject godless ways and worldly desires and to live self-controlled, upright, and godly lives in this present age, as we wait for the happy fulfillment of our hope in the glorious appearing of our great God and Savior, Jesus Christ. He gave himself for us to set us free from every kind of lawlessness and to purify for himself a people who are truly his, who are eager to do good" (Titus 2:11–14 NET).

A friend and mentor I call Counselor Frank says that this grace that motivates us is not necessarily a concept or even a merciful action but sometimes a Person. Because God's merciful action or amazing favor was literally the gift of his Son Jesus, I think Frank is right. Maybe I should capitalize Grace, the name that sometimes masquerades as a word, from here on out. Especially when I am talking about the Person. I don't want to cheapen Grace.

Dietrich Bonhoeffer, a German pastor and theologian, said in his writings of cheap grace versus costly grace: "Cheap grace is the preaching of forgiveness without requiring repentance, baptism without church discipline, communion without confession, absolution without personal confession . . . Costly grace is the treasure in the field; for the sake of it a man will gladly go and sell all that he has. It is the pearl of great price to buy which the merchant will sell all his goods . . . It is the call of Jesus Christ at which the disciple leaves his nets and follows him . . . Such grace is *costly* because it calls us to follow *Jesus Christ*. It is costly because it costs a man his life, and it is grace because it gives a man the only true life."[2]

Bonhoeffer said these things before he was martyred for the cause of Christ. He would not sell out and support his country's Nazi regime, which hid under nominal Christianity while attempting to physically take over the world and destroy the Jews. Instead, he spoke out against the demonic madness and was hanged just before the end of World War II.

Again, Jean Valjean was so changed by the grace given him after stealing the silverware that he became a new man and turned his life over to God. And like Valjean, I too have experienced God's grace in many ways and that has changed me, causing me to turn my mind, body, and Spirit over to the very being of God. I have found such a deep freedom in giving myself to him. And his grace sparked me to do so.

I think there is something very beautiful and mysterious

about the things that make up the very being of God. When we come into contact with his supernatural pardoning and receive what we don't deserve, we are literally sampling God and tasting his nature, which changes us. I believe that happens when the Holy Spirit covers us with a mixture of conviction and a helping hand after we fall to sin in our day. I think it happens when a Christian relies on God and truly forgives another without storing the offense and holding it to be played as a trump card at a later date.

As Brennan Manning indicated, all we have is thanks to the sheer bounty of God. As a result, I now find it easier to give and receive because it was first handed over to me by God and then by my wife. When I received the grace of God in my heart and held a little red-haired boy who knew my voice, I smiled a ginormous grin. I didn't simply hear about grace or talk about it; I felt it. When I did, it was amazing. It was Amazing Grayson!

6

A PAIR OF NAVY BLUE
KNEE-HIGH SOCKS

THE FIRST TIME I heard the popular expression, "You can't pol-ish a turd" was after a baseball game as I stood looking in a mirror, getting ready to comb my hair. I would have laughed a lot harder if the comment had not been directed at me. Nevertheless, I still chuckled. A little.

Pee-wee Herman responded to put-downs and name calling by cleverly asking, "I know you are, but what am I? I know you are, but what am I?"

I think that's a great question. Seriously.

In the early 1990s, Counselor Frank asked me something that was along the same line as Mr. Herman's.

He said, "Paul, who are you?"

After a few short seconds of wondering if I was dealing with a moron, I answered him rather arrogantly.

"You just said it. I'm Paul."

"No," he replied with a tiny chuckle. "That's your name."

"Oh," I said with a bit more respect. "If you put it that way, I guess I'm a baseball player."

"That's your job. That's not who you are."

"Oh, I got it. You mean like Catholic, Baptist, or Evangelical?"

"No. That would be your denominational preference."

I could feel my right hand pulling back my exposed king like a desperate man playing chess. I didn't want to move too quickly so I took some time before my next move. After a short stare off I let my tongue gently proceed.

"A male."

"No. That's your gender."

"I am now a single person who is going to be married to Kym?"

"No. Marital status."

"I am . . ."

"No."

"I am . . ."

"No."

I felt like rolling around on the floor, biting a stick, and screaming high-pitched cuss words while rabid foam began to drool from the corners of my mouth. I was mad! I was also twenty-two years old and didn't know who I was, which I supposed might be important in this life, possibly the whole point of it. Instead of being physically overdramatic, I just sat there and said the three words most people hate to say.

I said, "I don't know."

It was the first right answer I had given all day and I said it without screaming.

Shortly after I got into professional baseball, I had a pitching coach that offered few answers and liked to yell at me when

I pitched. At the time, I had poor control and walked a lot of people, which can make a holy bishop like the one who rescued Valjean kick in a stained-glass window. I understood that giving the batter a free pass wasn't the best thing for our team but I also couldn't figure out how to get my body to throw strikes. After I would walk a couple in a row, my pitching coach would walk out to the mound with my catcher and yell at the top of his lungs. I think he wanted the crowd to hear him.

"What the h—— are you doing? You gotta stop walking people, Byrd! You're wild! We need strikes not balls. We need to get some outs!"

After a couple of these meetings, I started to become embarrassed. Even my catcher would drop his head and look down at the ground. I felt like sarcastically replying, "Oh . . . Is that what I'm supposed to be doing? Throwing strikes? I thought you liked me walking people," but I didn't do that and instead just seemed to stand there nodding my head in agreement like I was getting something out of his nonconstructive criticism. Sad to say I was actually taking in a wound, one that said I was wild and stupid. Wild because I couldn't consistently throw strikes and stupid because I couldn't get my head to figure out how to make my right arm deliver them.

There is a time for yelling or smacking someone's bottom really hard, saying, "Come on, let's go, you're way better than that!" but this wasn't it. Those times are reserved for players who aren't paying attention or when someone gets lazy and halfheartedly jogs to back up a base. The truth of the matter is I would have responded much better if he would have helped me with his words and not torn me down. I tried to throw strikes. I wanted to throw strikes. But for some reason, I couldn't. And I desperately needed a former pitcher who had carried a ball and trudged up the hill before me to take me aside and show me how to conquer my wildness. I needed correct instruction. I needed someone to help me with my pitching mechanics and show me the right way to deliver a baseball. What I didn't need was the blind to lead the blind by heaping on condemnation.

The first time I read in the scriptures where God called me a saint, I yelled at him. I told him to "Take it back!"

He wouldn't.

God said, "My calling and gifts are irrevocable. Deal with it!"

But my sin is strong! I told him without using words. *Aren't you paying attention?*

God said to me, "Be careful. You shouldn't think of yourself more highly than you ought. The blood of my Son is stronger than your sin. Since his blood is good enough for me, his sacrifice should be good enough for you as well."

I sat quietly.

I felt as if I had insulted him. I had basically told God that I needed more than the blood of Jesus to cleanse me of my sin and more than the life offered through the resurrection for him to call me a saint. All of a sudden, I felt very prideful.

Sometimes it's tough to argue with our heavenly dad. I know that we can occasionally change his mind with our pleas, like Abraham did when God was going to immediately wipe out the city of Sodom, but there are certain things that you just can't budge him on. Identity is one of those things. He loves us too much.

The reason I looked up the word *saint* in the first place was due to the fact that Counselor Frank said that I was one and if I didn't believe him, I should just go home and start reading what God had said about me in the scriptures. I grabbed a few verses from him that pushed the identity issue and went home to prove him wrong. I couldn't.

The word *saint* literally means, holy one. And because I knew what I had done the night before and was increasingly troubled by the unholy thoughts that often assault my brain like a school of piranhas, I kept wondering silently to myself if God could be sued for false advertising. I had trouble accepting the sacred name tag because of my faulty behavior and I was confused by how a man crucified a couple millenniums ago could pay the penalty for something boneheaded that I was probably going to do tomorrow, as well as the condition I had found myself in from the very day I had been born. The problem and legacy of Adam.

For some reason, I thought real saints were people who no longer hang out in the physical world of earth; rather they graduated from this hellhole and only exist spiritually where they sit and sport soft neon halos glowing atop their half-invisible heads. They speak softly and talk about God's ways with complete certainty because they just finished playing golf with him on a course of tricky clouds. The saints don't go marching in, they already walked in through the pearly gates a long time ago and were changed upon their arrival. They went through a metal saint machine; a buzzer went off and they were instantly transformed. Then God notified a few churches here on earth where their images were put on necklaces and prayed to, in an effort to find lost items and cure diseases. That was them, this is me. It didn't make sense to me that true saints are people who still have the capability to live independently from God and sin. So I continued to wonder why the Apostle Paul called the Corinthian believers saints one minute and hammered them for all kinds of sins the next, including ones of a perverse sexual nature. I needed help.

I began to talk to God more and ask him if I understood what he said about me in the scriptures correctly. Gradually, I got it.

What I've learned over the years is that after we become Christians, we don't become saints because of something that we do but because of something that God did about two thousand years ago on the cross. The death and resurrection of Jesus is what changes people who want to receive him. And that's it! As far as our identity goes, our good and bad deeds do not establish who we are just as barking like a dog doesn't make me a hairy mongrel—being born of Lassie does. What I thought was so complex turned out to be so simple.

What did help change my behavior, however, was the fact that God encouraged me and called me fantastic names after he claimed me as his own. And the knowledge that I had already been transformed into a child of God despite my sometimes poor behavior released me from the weak image that I previously had of myself. I knew that I brought nothing to the table, but God did. What he walked in with and placed on the wood surface tasted pretty good and was very healing and changed my identity. I was amazed at who I had become, the names given me and other believers in Christ, which is where we all exist now and will always be since Jesus will never leave us. I read where he called me his child, his friend, a citizen of heaven, a member of a royal priesthood, a righteous man, a holy man, a minister of a new covenant, a new creation, a person who's been redeemed, a person who's been forgiven, and a saint. He said that I was his handiwork built by and created in his Son to shine like a star in a corrupt and depraved world. I learned from listening to the Spirit within me and reading the Bible that God's Son is the Saint Machine and we walk through his flashing radiance and are spiritually altered by simply believing in him.

Sure my flesh, or the part of me that wanted to live independently from God, still acted up but God said that he sees through my inadequacy in places where Jesus is present. All of a sudden, I felt transparent or something as if God was Superman and had X-ray vision that enabled him to look through me and divide the marrow from my soul checking out my spirit to notice Jesus. After continually reading about my identity that rested in God, I felt as if I was walking around holding some unseen treasure that was priceless. And I could now answer the question that Frank had originally asked without sounding like Pee-wee Herman. I was actually beginning to experience the solution of my sonship as a child of the King.

At times, Christianity seemed like a roller coaster to me. Before I came to Christ, I was often encouraged to embrace my sinfulness and separation from God. Then after paying attention to my behavior, I decided that what was said about me was true and I received brokenness by admitting to God that my heart was evil and my deeds repulsive. I began to feel wretched. I somehow realized that in and of myself I could offer him nothing. When God entered my heart and set me free, I was thankful, but mostly heard a similar message of being nothing but a poor old sinner saved by grace. I continued to get beaten down and I acted accordingly.

CONDEMNATION!

Some of the people that I had met in what I thought was real Christianity were sort of like the pitching coach that liked to scream at me and point the finger or my fellow classmate in college who said my writing was horrific. For every sermon that I heard on grace, I heard nine on how I needed to get it together. Fire and brimstone seemed to be not only for the godless but for all holy believers as well. After taking in the condemnation disguised as humility, I walked around like Eeyore, the pitiful donkey from *Winnie the Pooh*, until God worked through Frank to reveal and introduce me to the New Covenant, which is life after the cross and our adequacy as holy saints.

I learned to relax and trust that he who began a good work within me really would carry it on until the day of completion. It was not my job to continually focus on some sin-management program and try to look more like a super Christian holy man by living to please other people so they could see my fruit. Therefore, I started to focus on Jesus and I began to accept that I was a project who would always need him. I started to rest in the fact of who I had become in the eyes of God. His generous names for me made me respond to him and not become complacent. After all it was his kindness that led me to repentance in the first place and it was now his kindness mixed with grace that allowed me to walk. So just as I received him, I learned to walk with him. And I learned that his opinion of me was much better than the one I had of myself. Therefore, I began to live from him and not for him.

I must confess that I have not always come in first or even played baseball from this joyous perspective but I have been deeply moved by the power of God and even learned of his goodness during my own races.

One such occasion was in July 1998. I had a little over two years in the big leagues between the Atlanta Braves and New York Mets but really didn't do all that well. I had redefined the term bench warmer as I mostly sat and flicked sunflower seeds while my teammates did the real work on the field. As a result of poor control, I was sent down to the minors on three different occasions. One of the games I pitched for the Richmond Braves was against the Scranton Red Barons, the Triple-A affiliate for the Philadelphia Phillies. The great thing about this particular minor league game in Virginia was the reward waiting at the end. My pitching coach, Bill Fischer, had taken me aside before the game to tell me that if I showed that I was healthy, I would be traded to the Florida Marlins after the game. The Marlins had sent a scout to watch me pitch and I think he had a talk with my pitching coach and spilled the beans. I was not going to crack the rotation in Atlanta with names like Maddux, Glavine, and Smoltz on the backs of jerseys so those words were like fresh-squeezed lemonade to a parched man in the desert. My heart leapt.

I had already worked out the future details in my mind. After throwing a shutout, I would go to south Florida and buy a house. My wife and kids would love it there and I could be seen for years dominating the National League while the Atlanta Braves and New York Mets front office personnel could be seen sobbing on various sports channels murmuring, "We're sorry, we didn't know Paul was that good." So naturally I did what any solid Bible-believing Christian should do, I thanked God for being on the same page as me and got ready to pitch.

That night, in a tribute to the minor league players of yore, both teams had to wear the old-time scratchy wool jerseys from many years before. It was also a marketing gimmick. So in an effort to play along, I got the baggiest pair of pants that I could find and pulled up my socks to my knees. I didn't mind looking like the men at the turn of the century and the players who are seen on crackling highlight reels throwing and lifting their leg in rapid fashion while organ music sounds off in the background. After all I was in a fabulous mood now that God had heard and answered my prayer. This was the day the Lord had made! Hosanna in the highest!

Before the first pitch, I was excited to see my family checking me out from the first row in the stands. My wife Kym was juggling Colby in her arms. He was almost a year old. When he got a few years older and the beer men would walk down the aisles shouting "Cold beer here!" Colby would always look at them thinking they were calling his name, so he would turn his head and shout, "What? Stop yelling at me!" It was hilarious. Even though our family is much older now, we still laugh together when we hear that familiar phrase from the man who walks down the aisles of the stadium carrying a large tray of ale. In unison, we all look over at Colby, waiting for a response. He just sits there and smiles.

Grayson, who was two years old at the time, sat in the seat next to them anxiously watching me, his dad. It always amazed me that he would sit through nine innings and truly enjoy the game at such a young age. He wouldn't move. He treasured baseball and delighted in home runs. Even when I gave them up. He was the only voice heard in our family section that could be found cheering and clapping for the other team when they hit a round tripper. He just liked the crack of the bat. I thought that was great. He was innocent and he was mine.

Anyway, I gave up seven runs that memorable summer night and lasted only four innings. I yielded home run after base hit after home run. My fastball rarely reached the speed necessary to crack a teacup and to make matters worse I walked five batters, showing the Marlins scout that I had poor control. Grayson had a lot to cheer about that evening, just nothing to clap for concerning me. It was easily my worst minor league performance ever. My manager took me out of the game and I walked off the field to human silence and a chorus of chirping crickets. I tried to hold my head up high knowing that I was a child of God. But that didn't even work. To be honest, I felt like the guy my friend joked about in the mirror, I felt like a turd.

I walked over and sat on the bench in our dugout. I really liked my pitching coach, Bill Fischer, but even he seemed at a loss for any real words.

"When are you going to start throwing strikes?" he asked.

I just sat there.

I remember getting undressed in the locker room that night and pulling down my high socks. I had never worn them like that and I wondered if looking like a clown with my high socks and baggy pants had anything to do with why I had pitched so poorly.

On the way home, I punched the radio hard not caring if I did any real damage to my hand or not. I never knew if I would ever get another shot at the big leagues again. A person only gets so many chances. And many get none. I had gotten another opportunity that night and I had blown it.

When I arrived and entered our small apartment, I looked at my beautiful wife and displayed an emptiness that would make most corpses appear vivacious. Kym on the other hand had a great big smile on her face, one that I wanted to wipe off. Apparently she didn't get the memo that this was a time for mourning. A time for ashes, sackcloth, and head shaving.

"I want to show you something," she said excitedly. "Follow me."

And with those words she led me into the bedroom where my oldest son Grayson was sleeping. She pulled back the covers to encourage me in a way that no friend or holy man could ever impart to me through words. My son had gone through a dresser drawer, put on some socks, and pulled them up over his pajamas. He told her that he would not go to bed until he looked just like his daddy. He wanted to be me. He wanted to wear high socks.

When I looked upon him that night with a lumpy throat and tears running down my cheeks, I gained a little more freedom into the things of God. I experienced what it must feel like to God when we want to reflect our Father in a world of people that mostly point their finger at him for not getting on their program or allowing pain in the daily games of this world. Grayson was a little me and he wanted to show it. Ever since I first asked Jesus into my life, I wanted to be like God. But I quickly dismissed the idea because I thought that type of thinking was for arrogant people and beings who wore white straitjackets in padded asylums. But after I learned about my identity, the grace given me through Christ and looking at a long pair of socks on my son's legs, I decided that it must feel pretty good to our Father and our God when we desire to be like them. I don't want you to confuse me with a real cult member, or any person who says that man can become what God is now. That is heresy. I am not saying that and we can't. But I do want you to hear that we can become like him and possess his character without attaining his deity. I have always wanted to be godly. I have always wanted to be holy because that is the character of my Father in heaven. Let's face it, most boys want to be like their dad and I am no different. As a performing athlete and a common churchgoer, I just thought his holiness was something to be pursued and chased after, not received. Again, I thought life and what I made of myself was up to me and my own effort. I bought into the often-taught Christian treadmill of performing for acceptance instead of from it. As a guy, that made sense to me even though it's not God's way. I guess I'm used to coaches telling me what to do and getting on it right away. Earning something. I didn't know that God was going to coach me by encouraging me through my failures and simply changing my name to call out his Son who had already done the work and had made his home deep inside my Spirit.

God polished a turd that night. Yes, sir. He made it very shiny. He used disappointment and baseballs. But it glistened the most when he used my son and swabbed it back and forth with a pair of navy blue knee-high socks.

I saw the change in my perspective when I once helped coach a young boy into healing while teaching him how to properly throw a baseball. The boy's name was Brandon. He was very tall and had long arms, which should have allowed him to get some whip on his fastball but the expected velocity never came out. He just threw the ball at about half speed getting uncomfortable every time I asked him to turn up the heat. I prayed as I was talking to him and I got revelation into his problem.

"Are you afraid to throw hard because you might hit somebody?"

His head immediately dropped and he got choked up.

"Can you look at me?" I asked.

Brandon's father spoke up from the background telling me that he hit somebody in the head the year before and the batter lay on the ground for a few minutes until he was walked off the field with the help of the other team's coaches.

"After that, he has never wanted to pitch," his father said.

"Hey, man," I said to Brandon. "Did you try to hit the batter on purpose?"

"No!" he emphatically replied, as if he were defending himself.

"Well, then, what are you worried about? It's your job to pitch inside and it's the hitter's job to get out of the way if you miss. You didn't mean to hurt anybody. In fact you didn't do anything wrong. The batter is not going to feel bad if he hits one up the middle and you have to duck."

"I know," he said, "but I'm going to just keep on hitting people. I'm wild."

"Who told you that?"

"Everybody has."

I smiled. I called his father closer to me wanting to teach them both at the same time. I have always believed that baseball is about mentoring and fatherhood. When I teach, I want the student's biggest supporter right there with me so I can hopefully coach myself out of a job. A boy needs to connect with his father.

"To be honest, I don't know if you're wild or not. I do know that at your point of release you pull your head way off to the left. Your eyes are looking down somewhere between home and first base. It's hard to throw strikes when you're checking out some green grass that's ten feet away instead of the catcher's mitt."

"Okay, so what do I need to do?" Brandon asked.

"First you need to fix your eyes on the glove. Don't let them leave it. Then take a deep breath from your gut. Really deep. It will help you relax. After that I want you to take your head straight to the target while keeping your eyes on it until the ball hits the glove. Your arm and body will do the rest."

Brandon gave it a try. After throwing about seven out of ten pitches for strikes, he started to smile right along with me. His shoulders began to lighten and straighten up and his body language told me that he was starting to enjoy what he was doing.

After he threw a pitch in the dirt, I said, "Who cares? Only Jesus is perfect." Brandon smiled again.

I made him stop in the middle of his lesson to teach him another one. My eyes grew intense and I asked him to look right at their blueness. "Hey!" I said. "Do you still think you're wild?"

"No," he replied.

"Neither do I. Whoever told you that was full of sh——! They didn't know what they were talking about. You're not wild, you're turning into a man and when you look at your target like you're supposed to you have great control!"

I'm not sure why a curse word was necessary at that particular moment; I hadn't seriously cursed in a long time. It just rolled off my tongue with ease probably as a by-product of great passion and pain. I usually don't think clearly during those seconds in my life but God still uses my occasional rough edges. I followed my words with a handshake and Brandon wouldn't let go. I assume he thought that I had set him straight that night but in reality he had healed me in some strange way by letting me serve him.

I watched him pitch in a game a few nights later and he dominated. He threw hard and he threw strikes. I cried while driving home. God used that young boy who was turning into a man to mend an open incision in me that I thought had already closed up a long time ago. Maybe God just reopened a scar and worked through a tender time of my life to do a better job of sewing it up. Whichever it was, I don't know. I just know that God is the ultimate cardiologist and I gained freedom from that whole experience. I was also thankful that I had fallen down many times and lived in areas of wildness so that I could interact with God and offer my strength to help Brandon find his control.

God is so good to me. He is so good to me that he found an

unusual way to transform me from a turd to a saint. Although I was once embarrassed about this heavenly title, I have now come to accept it because it is a gift from God and one that came at a huge price for him. Therefore, I have learned to think of myself and smile while having a grateful heart. I think I am most thankful every time I get ready to pitch and reach down to my ankles pulling up a pair of navy blue knee-high socks.

LARRY THE LEGEND

IN 1999, the year after my fateful start against Randy Johnson, I got to dress next to him on the National League All-Star Team in the Fenway Park locker room. When we shook hands, I felt like I was looking at a totem pole with a fancy mullet, one that reminded me of my hair back in college. He was more intimidating up close and I wondered how many times he had hit his head while walking through doorways.

Bruce Bochy, the Padres' manager who captained the National League's team, selected me to be on his pitching staff for that midsummer classic in Boston. In less than one year, I went from getting bombed in Triple A and failing to stay on a major league roster to having a locker next to some of the greatest players in the world.

Hours after I walked into the clubhouse, I pulled up my high red Philadelphia socks, put on my uniform, and sat on the freshly cut green grass about ten feet away from home plate to watch the home run contest. My son Grayson Byrd sat on my lap and we watched Mark McGwire hit towering home runs over the left-field Green Monster that headed out toward the famous neon Citgo sign. The white baseballs literally vanished out into the steamy darkness. Grayson chuckled with excitement at each crack of the bat and pressed his back against my chest as the famous St. Louis Cardinal known as Big Red hit about fifteen of the most spectacular fly balls that I had ever seen. Near the end of the exhibition, Jim Thome, a great power hitter from the American League, dropped to his knees and began to raise his arms up and down in a worshipful fashion. Respect!

Ken Griffey, Jr., a tremendous hitter from the American League, won the contest that night, but to be honest I thought that Mark McGwire stole the show. After the smoke cleared, Big Red grabbed a black Sharpie marker and signed a jersey for Grayson right there in the locker room. After his name, he wrote the number seventy. It signified the amount of home runs in a season that he had hit the year before to break the long-standing record of the big-gunned Roger Maris.

The next night was equally chilling as Kevin Costner introduced the All-Century Team to the baseball-crazed Boston fans. He called out names like Johnny Bench, Hank Aaron, Carl Yastrzemski, Tom Seaver, and Say Hey Willie Mays. All of the legends stood out on the infield surface receiving praise from standing fans of all ages who were screaming and sounding off horns.

You could feel a volcano-like tension at the end of the ceremony when Kevin Costner announced that he had one name left to call. After a few moments, he raised his voice to a new level and introduced Ted Williams, calling him the greatest hitter of all time. Even though a near standing Hank Aaron could have protested that statement, I think everyone knew it was a comment designed to honor Ted Williams in his final days at his own Fenway Park. The Boston fans erupted and shook the stadium to a force probably not felt since Carlton Fisk's famous arm-waved World Series home run against the Reds in 1975.

Ted Williams entered the stadium on a golf cart from a large green curtain in centerfield. He rounded the warning track and met all the players at the center of the baseball diamond. Players like Tony Gwynn and George Brett who knew Ted personally and had apparently worked with him walked over as tears fell down the Splendid Splinter's face. I just sat back a few feet away and clapped my hands as I watched Ted Williams struggle to get out of the golf cart and stand to greet everybody. I felt like some crazy fan that had bought a uniform in the gift shop and slipped onto the field, undetected by the heavy security.

The Splendid Splinter couldn't stand by himself anymore and he could not stop crying in appreciation at one of the last and greatest moments of his storied career. I thought of the day at the White House when I had seen Mr. Williams stand in confidence and hold his head high while being honored by President Bush. Now, after a time, the Splinter looked more like the Great DiMaggio when he used a slower hand to sign my baseball. DiMaggio had died a few months earlier and I thought of the years that had quickly passed since the days we all stood for a picture. I had gotten married, fathered two boys, and begun to establish myself as a starter in the big leagues. The Silent Voice who lived in my heart had gotten louder over those years as I welcomed the wisdom and discernment that came from him. My questions over purpose and significance had been answered since that day I stared at the American flag on the executive lawn. For me, it would be found only in Christ and walking with him and there was freedom in discovering my purpose.

I also thought of baseball in that prized moment and my two

boys who had my blood running through them. I thought of my earthly dad who taught me how to hold a two-seam fastball on an empty field across the street from our house in Louisville. I thought about Kevin Costner and the film *Field of Dreams*, a movie about fatherhood cleverly disguised behind the mask of baseball. Suddenly, I wanted to leave one of the greatest moments of my life and play catch in some backyard sandlot with my dad. I wanted to go back to Louisville and be ten years old all over again. I wanted to sit on my father's lap and steer the car down our old street, named Ledyard Road, and turn it into the crumpled driveway that faced our garage.

CONNECTIONS

My earthly father is named Larry Byrd. Even though he didn't play for the Celtics, I introduce him as the *real* Larry Byrd or Larry the Legend. People laugh. When he and my mother visited us for those magical few nights in the crowded and historic city of Boston, I dropped his name to one of the restaurant managers in hopes of getting us a table. I said to the headwaiter, "Hey, I need a table for Larry Byrd. Do you have anything available?"

It worked and there was instant confusion as a couple of waiters scurried like field mice to get something ready. The mass preparation was followed by laughter when they saw my father walk around the corner and I said, "Here he is!" I guess my version of Larry the Legend was a little different from the one of most Celtic fans.

Even though my father is retired, he still manages to work in various nonpaid professions. Not only is he a comedian but also a master drywall painter, philosopher, and spaghetti maker. I have to admit that his spaghetti casserole is pretty darn good. He uses Karo pancake syrup in the sauce, which sounds nasty but actually flavors the dish quite well. My nephew Rick Ridge doesn't like the curious sauce because it has mushrooms but he avoids telling anybody. He just sits there and smiles a sheepish grin at me. Because the Legend is somewhat sensitive, he doesn't want to hurt my dad's feelings.

The hardest person to tell I had become a Christian was my father. And I don't know why. I do know that my father has always had good intentions with me. He just didn't have much to draw from. Growing up he was not allowed to speak unless spoken to first and thus he felt invisible. His dad, my grandfather, had no relationship with him and died when my father was fifteen. Until I did a family tree Cub Scout project with my son Colby, I never even knew my grandfather's name. I had to call my dad and ask him. There was tension. Honestly, I think it hurt for my dad to even say his father's name over the phone. So I guess my father grew up damaged. Like most people, he tried to do his best. He spent a lot of time with me throwing baseballs in the backyard, rebounding numerous basketballs, and running wide receiver patterns as we took turns throwing the football. To this day, I have never beaten him in a game of horse. He shoots the old-fashioned, one-legged set shot swishing the basketball regularly. I will probably have to wait for him to get into a wheelchair before I can take him. As Colby says, "If Paw Paw shoots from the corner, we're dead meat!"

The last thing I want to sound like I am doing is bashing my earthly father. I am not. It is written that "love covers a multitude of sins," and I have always felt deeply cared for by my father even when it wasn't perfect. I admired him and always felt his love, mainly because he spent time with me. A father spending time with his son is so important. I would not be successful in the sports arena today if it weren't for my father taking an interest in me and learning my bent. There were hours and hours of his life that he used up on me during the summers in Louisville. When it became apparent that baseball was in my heart, he went out and bought a book by Tom Seaver called *The Art of Pitching* because he knew little about my favorite sport. Quite often, my father would take me to McDonald's for an Egg McMuffin, followed by a little pitching and batting practice at St. Matthew's Little League. Today, when I stand on the fields in many stadiums and smell the grass while biting the leather string on my glove, I think of my father and the times that we spent together. He was my hero as a young boy and even now as an adult, I look up to him in many different ways.

I learned from a show titled *Raising Cain* on PBS that 40 percent of American children grow up without any interaction from their biological father. It is the highest percentage of any industrialized nation. After spending so much time with my dad, learning that statistic was very sad for me.

Many times the dads who are still in the home have to travel. The most heartbreaking thing Grayson ever said to me was when he was about four years old. He asked me, "Hey, Dad, does your other family have as good toys as we have?" I felt like someone hit me with a sledgehammer. I had to explain to him that every time our team plane takes off I am going to work. He smiled. His comment prompted me to start taking him to the field a little more often, even if it changed my workout schedule or caused me to rearrange a few video meetings.

Even though I have always thought highly of my father, at

times he has really hurt our family. It's very tough to talk about and I will not break confidences in our family for the sake of a book but in short he has struggled in a few different areas. And it's not only him. We've all had our problems with communication, anger, and handling conflict. We've made mistakes in the past. This includes me. It's gotten so that people take turns not talking to each other in my family and we make alliances until something outlandish happens and we all switch positions on our family mobile in hopes of somehow coming back into balance. I understand that at times some space is needed and at other times it is not. I never really know what to do anymore. Mostly, I just get confused and stand around the table at Thanksgiving feeling sad, rubbing my temple with my index finger wondering why people are missing and how things get so out of whack. Since even Jesus had problems with his family when he hung out in Nazareth, I guess I can't get too upset. Maybe there is a fellowship with God to be had in the midst of it all.

I have chewed many times on a passage in the seventeenth chapter of Acts that says God has specifically put us in his family of choice for us at his specific time for us here on earth. God says he does so for our benefit, that we may become frustrated and have a chance to reach out to him. I guess that's why all families seem to be dysfunctional at some level. So we hurt and look to God for parental advice and healing. Pain makes sense to me now. Strange to say but I now see some pain as a gift. Nobody in the history of the world has had to live my life and no one else ever will. Therefore, I have learned to thank God for the wounds that he has structured this world to give me—the people in my life that have caused me to run to him. I like to talk about those scars now and sometimes display them with pride. No longer covering them up, I am very thankful that God has put me in my family. I love my parents and our somewhat damaged family tree very much.

I am also not so arrogant to think that I have not given out a few gashes myself, especially to the ones I love. I am aware that I have wielded a knife, mostly my tongue, and hurt people. I hope the cuts aren't too deep. Over the years, I have learned to talk in softer tones with my wife and two boys but I would be lying to say I am perfect. Every now and then I catch myself yelling without even knowing it. I have also learned to apologize to my kids after I blow it. Telling someone you are wrong and sorry for your actions goes a long way. So far they have always been quick to forgive me.

In December 2002, *USA Today* featured an article about "The Psychology of Happiness." The article focused on a study that only examined people who were happy. The number-one characteristic of those who enjoy their lives and are truly happy was forgiveness. In other words, happy people can forgive. I guess handing out a pardon to someone with your heart and really meaning it, is very liberating. I have begun to experience that. Forgiving and loving my earthly father despite his shortcomings and failures has been one of the greatest feelings that I have ever come to experience. It has been very healing, a pure salve that has covered my heart.

Dr. Tom Robbins, a counselor from Kentucky, once told me a cool story about Prince Henry of Portugal, better known in our history books as Henry the Navigator. It was the prince's lifelong ambition to discover an all-water route around Africa that reached the Far East. Using a compass, Prince Henry started by traveling south down the coast of Africa. Because they took a limited amount of supplies, ships would leave a marker at their farthest point of travel and turn back. They would gather more supplies and return months later to sail past that point and forge into new waters. The men who had each gone before them had enabled the ones who would follow to be able to go a little farther. This process went on for years until one day, after thirty or more voyages, the ship was loaded up one last time and in a final voyage, they made it to the Far East.

That has been my father. For reasons that deal with a lack of supplies, he has taken the ship as far as he can take it. I have always admired the fact that my father tried to do a better job with me than his father did with him. My father was dragged off to school having never picked up a pencil so he made sure that I was better equipped in the skills of mathematics. I could do long division by the time I walked into the first grade. My father had a stuttering problem when he was young so he asked me questions at the dinner table making sure that I would speak and learn to organize my thoughts and say them properly with my mouth. I became well spoken and did my first television interview at the age of ten at a University of Kentucky baseball camp. Even now, if someone compliments me on being a popular interviewee, I think of my dad and his encouragement. There were early years when he drank too much alcohol but he beat the problem and I have always been very proud of him for that. He also made sure that I never went down the same trail because he knew firsthand the problems it could lead to. Again, he is my hero.

So, like Prince Henry's strategy, I have appreciated my father's map in my life as a person who has gone before me and now I want to try to go the whole way and make it to my own little version of the Far East in fatherhood. This statement is tough because I'm not sure a person in this life ever fully arrives. I guess what I'm trying to say is that I want to give my best and finish strong as a father. I hope I don't get shipwrecked. I'm sure I will need the advice of a person who can multiply fish and calm the storms along the way, especially if I am to go the distance.

Larry the Legend was a police officer in Louisville during the civil rights era. Black people were unjustly persecuted during those times, being forced to use different bathrooms than men and women with white skin, having to go to certain restaurants and separate schools. Even water fountains and parks were segregated. Muhammad Ali, the great heavyweight champion from Louisville, claimed to have thrown his gold medal from the 1960 Olympics in the Ohio River when he returned from the games and was thrown out of a restaurant.

My father was a sergeant in the homicide division and was in charge of organizing cases and trying to solve over ninety murders a year. He went days without sleep and for a time was rarely home. I met a local judge who had silver hair one night in a bar. He said my father was the best police officer in the history of the force. He meant it and I smiled. It made me proud. But as a policeman, my father experienced a lot. Maybe too much. I thought it was some kind of cool as a young boy when he would tell me about shootings. I remember my mom putting a ban on the manslaughter stories fearing that they were too graphic for me. But I used to beg him for more. He would let a few accounts slip by though, when it was just him and me, and I sat on his lap driving our family's green station wagon down some private street. Those stories were under her radar, of course. I guess most kids like hearing about blood in great amounts and I was no different.

Sadly, the real Larry Byrd once told me that in all his years on the police force the two most crooked professions he ran across were the religious organizations and law enforcement. I suspect that all lines of work are fallen and less than perfect. Maybe he just expected better behavior from people that signed up to help. He has also told me that every person who is breathing cares only about money. I don't like to use words like *always* and *never* or other hairy adverbs that don't leave room for error but as life has gone by, I've definitely understood his point.

Growing up, the Legend told me time and time again that he couldn't stand people who were dogmatic. Finally as a teenager I had to look up the word to find out that my father was the most dogmatic person that I knew. That puzzled me. I realized that sometimes people point out the faults in others that they don't like about themselves. I fight against the same qualities in myself and I pray to see the boards in my own eyes before I talk about others' specks. I'm getting better.

On occasion, I would try to use my father's clout with the neighborhood kids. I think even Jesus told the nonbelieving Pharisees in the end, "My dad is going to beat up your dad," so I presume I wasn't all that bad. I remember walking back from the convenience store and telling Chris Lynch, a childhood friend of mine, that my father was going to take him down to the station and lock him up for stealing that two-cent Mary Jane piece of candy. Immediately, he got nervous and handed it to me. It was quite delicious.

I don't mean any disrespect to my elders. I want to honor them. But I think, as you get older, you become a little more set in your ways. I'm not sure if you have gotten tired of everyone telling you what to do all your life or if you're upset at all the wrong information you've received over the years. I don't know which it is, maybe neither. I've also noticed that as life goes by, people either gravitate to their upbringing and become their parents without knowing it, or they take a blood oath to do everything differently. In other words, if they were raised in an extremely strict environment they become part-time hippies as parents and more of a relaxed friend to their children. And vice versa. I suppose becoming different might be growth. Or maybe we all just live in cycles. Whatever goes on it seems that the pendulum rarely stops in the middle. At what age do we realize we have become our parents? If we do at all. I want my pendulum to slow down. I pray to have balance.

One time while driving down Shelbyville Road, after my first year of pro baseball, I threw some Jesus at the Legend mentioning some of my favorite wisdom, "How about when Jesus said, 'Do unto others as you would have them do unto you'?"

He responded by saying, "I could have said that!"

It seems to me that my father takes a certain pride in being pessimistic even though he claims that his remarks hang out in the world of realism. I don't know if he delights in being that way or if he has just had a tough life and not wanted to change. Either way, I still love him. And I have always appreciated his real and honest answers.

I have asked my father about heaven several times only to hear that he doesn't want to go there. It's pretty strange. When I questioned him why, he answered by saying, "Let's say I want to play pool in heaven and I go to break with the cue ball. I don't want all the balls to go in the pockets. Sometimes, I want to scratch. I want a second shot. Everything is not supposed to always go your way . . . It also sounds boring to sit on a soft downy cloud, sing worship music, and pluck a harp all day long."

I really didn't know what to say to that philosophy, which in his mind had Plato and Aristotle looking like morons. I certainly didn't think of heaven as being a boring worship service and I didn't feel that we would be void of our emotions or walk around with the Midas touch. I did think that heaven involved a Person. I took a different route with him not knowing if Satan offered tougher pool shots in hell or not.

"Dad," I said. "What about heaven the Person? You know, being with Jesus. God as a loving parent and all that sort of stuff? Does that interest you?"

"I don't think so," my father replied. "He seems too dogmatic to me. Everyone has to receive Jesus? If God can't accept other people and me just the way I am, then I don't want to be around him either. Why do I have to change? The h—— with him!" As I noted with an exclamation point, he said this emphatically and I was sad.

Men's Health once listed the top things you discover after turning thirty. Number one was discovering that your father isn't such an a——h—— after all. I laughed when I first read that. Then I was still. I guess when kids come and the stress of life beats you down you learn to give a little more grace knowing that you're not perfect either. I never thought my dad was the posterior end of the alimentary canal, I just became increasingly critical of him as I grew into my teen years and beyond, which sort of backfired in my face when I grew up and realized that I was really complaining about myself.

It reminds me of the line in *To Kill a Mockingbird* when Gregory Peck says that to know a man you have to get in his shoes and walk around a bit. As I've gotten older, I have noticed that my shoes have holes in them too and ones that are similar to the Legend's. I call them hand-me-downs. I suppose that's because I have gone down trails that my father has walked and I've followed in a few of his footsteps without even knowing it. At times, I try to put on a pair of new shoes and go in a different direction but for some strange reason I look down and notice that I'm still wearing the same old clodhoppers. I guess I find their comfort to be compelling. I'm glad Jesus offers Shoe Goo.

Ben, my friend the writer, once reminded me about the time Ted Turner received an honorary PhD from Harvard. The great media mogul stepped up to the microphone to address the crowd and before beginning his speech, he looked skyward and said, "Is that good enough, Dad?" Ben found it amazing that regardless of all Turner's accolades such as winning the prestigious America's Cup in yachting, owning several sports franchises, building a worldwide television network, and trading with the New York Mets to acquire Paul Byrd, he still felt driven by the expectations of his deceased father. Obviously, Mr. Turner's dad had a huge impact on his life, one that went way beyond the passing down of a billboard business and a struggling television station. I'm sure that his father's death was very hard for him.

One of the most emotional moments for me as a Christian came when I discovered that my earthly father had shaped my view of my heavenly one. In the early nineties, Counselor Frank had me fill out an examination about the real Larry Byrd. It was a multiple-choice survey that asked questions such as, "How close do you feel to your father?" and "Does your father constantly bring up your shortcomings?" and "Is your father proud of you?"

I don't enjoy tests. My entire life has seemed like one. So I was thrilled when he told me that there were no wrong answers and the only stipulation was that I had to be honest. I like authenticity. I grabbed a number-two pencil and tried to be it.

A week after turning in my spiritual homework, Counselor

Frank asked if I felt the same way about God that I did my earthly father. When I chuckled and replied with an emphatic, "No!" Frank responded by laying my answers on a transparency. My test was now up on a wall. I told you I hate tests. Anyway, he placed another test I had taken and mailed in from minor league baseball about three months prior. That test was similar but not exactly the same. My mind came to a crashing halt when I realized that I had taken a previous survey about God with the same questions just reworded a bit. I had been tricked. I was without a straitjacket and there was no bright light but I sure felt uncomfortable. Back in that itchy skin I had as a kid. Once again, I needed lotion. Counselor Frank, now looking like Ming the Merciless or some famous torture specialist, asked me if I wanted him to overlap the two plastic sheets. I looked down at the ground.

"No," I replied softly. I already knew. I was wrong. My denial had been defeated.

Frank led me through steps of freedom. I had to confess blasphemy. I was worshipping a false God. I kept looking up with open arms like Ted Turner saying, "Is that good enough, Dad?" I guess there have been many times in this life when I have been trying to please my earthly father without even knowing it, hoping to see a smile on the former policeman's face. Similar to Dan Fogelberg, a great lyrical musician, I had spent most of my life imitating my living legacy, Larry the Legend, by being a good, honest, and just person apart from Christ, which is impossible. Because my dad was the leader of our band, his physical blood ran through me. And until that moment, I had no idea just how much I looked up to him and how much his lessons had sculpted my soul. Instantly, I knew I needed to run to God.

"Don't feel bad," Counselor Frank explained. "Nine out of ten people I work with feel the same way."

You see for some unknown cosmic reason most people see God the Father in light of the earthly father who raised them. Or the one who didn't and should have. That's their view of God. If they were abandoned as a child then their God is faraway and not caring as an adult. If their father was tough and critical then God becomes a strict judge always shaking a finger. If they had a great mother and she was their primary caretaker, that needs to be dealt with as well. No one is without fault in his or her love. And unfortunately we weren't designed for anything less than God's unconditional love. Even a fantastic parent can't fill that void. Just as your stomach was made for food so your spirit was made for God. Because my father spent a lot of time with me, deep down I had no choice but to think this was the character of the person that Jesus had rescued me to. It wasn't Larry Byrd's fault. Just like all of us, he is not perfect. He had done what every kid wants, he had tried. This is why from the day that my two boys could under-stand English I have told them that I will fail them as a father—in the life-giving sort of way. I'm sorry they have to look somewhere else for perfection, but they do. I have pointed them to God as their true dad. As they get older and the storms come, I hope they take me up on that offer and rely on him. I deeply desire that they know and trust God while giving him true thanksgiving in the trials. And when the sunshine is bright in their lives, I hope they notice their true Father and receive his favor as well with the same gratitude.

But as for me, I needed a get-out-of-jail-free card and I got one that day in Frank's office. I learned that God was my father.

Later that evening, before I opened my Bible, I said a prayer to my heavenly father that felt somewhat sappy but honest. My prayer was this: "Dad, I am starting over. I want to pick up this book and know more about you. I'm tired of studying it. I have had enough of textbooks. I don't want to stock up on knowledge or continue to memorize verses that I think I understand. I am tired of comparing myself with others and their knowledge as well. I want to be a one-year-old and start all over again learning about you and your character. Talk to me, please. Tell me about yourself. When I open this Bible please teach me about my sonship and your Fatherhood. Teach me how you feel about me. Please."

Regardless of the words that came out of my mouth, my heavenly Father knew my heart was seeking him. Over the years God has answered that prayer. I have truly experienced him as an internal and eternal spiritual Father.

Speaking of fathers, I have a good friend who looks like the actor, Andy Garcia, named Russ Ortiz. We played together for two years in Atlanta. Our lockers were next to each other, which proved to be a good fit. Russ didn't say much but when he did it was sort of like E. F. Hutton: everyone stopped to listen.

He recently told me a marvelous story that emotionally took me back to those powerful minutes in Frank's office. When Russ was one and his brother about three, his earthly father abandoned them. His mother was an overworked police officer in the Los Angeles area, which meant Russ and his brother spent many a night with their grandparents. He longed to see his biological father but no one came knocking on the door to take him out to a movie, teach him how to bait a fishing hook, or play a game of catch. One day after a baseball game in high school, an unusual man had stood by the fence and stared at both of them as they made their way past him. Russ and his brother sat in the backseat of the car as their mother drove away from the parking lot. After a few minutes passed, their mom informed them that the man who had been looking intently into the car through the side window was their father. Unable to go back, that portion of time stands as the only memory Russ has of his biological father. Because his father knew where to find him, Russ always had questions that floated around his head while growing up and wondered if his earthly father was secretly watching him pitch like that day in high school when he stood from afar.

The beautiful ending to the story is not that Russ reunited with the man who stared through the car window, because up until now he hasn't. No. Instead, my friend told me how he claimed Christ as his life in college after getting honest about his sin and feelings of inadequacy. Russ told me that learning the fatherhood aspect of the gospel answered the longing question in his brain about whether or not his father was secretly in attendance.

"Now, Paul," Russ said to me with robust eyes, "at that moment, after hearing that God was my real dad, I knew my Father was at all my games watching and cheering for me. Even now he watches! And that is something that I have always wanted and desperately needed."

Earthly fathers don't have to be perfect, just there. All most children want is for their fathers and parents to love them, spend time with them, and build into them. And if you ask Russ, God does that, he appears in his own way.

Through the years, I have learned a lot about God and his scandalous goodness. But nothing that I have learned has ever awed me more than his gracious favor given at the cross, that when received, made me his child. Nothing!

Please understand that this is my message to anyone who will listen. This is what burns deep in the core of me. That God is desperately in love with you. He is all consumed with becoming your Father and repairing a relationship once lost. He wants you to become his daughter or son. If you already have, he wants you to know him deeper, experience him fuller, and live from him now instead of later.

According to the Bible, pure religion is looking after orphans and widows (James 1:27). The band called Sixpence None the Richer titled one of their CDs *The Fatherless and the Widow*. I get pictures in my head when a word is thrown out to me. If someone says the word orphan I see the baby Oedipus wrapped in a towel high on the rocks waiting to die. Or Mowgli getting carried off by a pack of wolves. I think of abandonment. I feel it. When it comes to a widow, my brain usually flashes up an image similar to that of an elderly woman staggering with a cane. At any rate when those two words are brought up in conversation I rarely think of or get a picture myself. But that is what we are, all orphans, all widows. All kicked out and abandoned by the fall, needing to be filled by that which only God can fill and that with himself.

I once watched a made-for-television movie about the life of Steven Stayner, a boy who was abducted at the age of seven by a self-proclaimed Protestant minister. It was called *I Know My First Name Is Steven*, because at some point the young boy who was taken realizes that most of his life has been a lie and the only thing he remembers that is true about himself is literally his first name, Steven. When the child predator abducts another boy, Steven calls the police and they rescue him. Soon after he is watching his own story on the news and sees his original family on the television screen and he knows that his parents are coming to get him. It is a tense-filled moment when it becomes apparent to Steven that he must walk out to the curb and get picked up to meet his real family. I can't imagine the thoughts going through this young boy's head. At that moment, a divided boy needed a father to run to for advice. But he was alone. Would his real dad be pleased with the sight of his long-lost son? I was miserable over that movie. I hurt for that little boy. Then I realized that he was akin to all of us. We are all sort of Steven Stayners on the inside, it's just that some of us don't know it.

Again, the gospel of the New Testament is presented in such a way that it is almost like realizing that we have each been abducted as a child and what the world teaches us apart from Christ is not the truth. We find out by watching the news or hearing from a friend or reading the Bible that God is coming to get us soon and quickly. Do we want to go? Or make a quick last-ditch effort into the woods to live life as a runaway, because someone told us we would have to play the harp for God, a person we wrongly feel abandoned us and who we believe from poor life examples is unaccepting?

I know. I am walking out to the curb. I can't wait for him to come and pick me up and that in fullness.

RIGHT: Hugging Mom in 1984. Dad helped coach me at St. Matthew's. His socks were falling down.

BELOW: Spring break in seventh grade. This is the first time I saw the ocean. Notice the abs. I was totally ripped!

I played basketball for St. Xavier and posed for this shot in 1985.

Standing between Lisa Carpenter and Amy Adelberg
on eighth-grade graduation day at Sacred Heart.
Sister Catherine is hiding behind my right shoulder.

Soaking my left foot with my maternal grandmother.
My grandfather is in the background. He had an amazing reputation
as a Christian and would give you the shirt off his back.

Pitching for St. Xavier
against Louisville Male my sophomore year.

RIGHT: Kneeling in right field in my freshman year at LSU. Notice Tiger Stadium in the background. It's one of the loudest places to watch a game and is nicknamed Death Valley.
(Used by permission of the LSU Athletic Department)

BELOW: Winning the College World Series in 1991.
(Used by permission of the LSU Athletic Department)

LEFT: Wayne, the guy who sounded like a cult member to me when he first shared the Gospel. I'm glad he lived in a neighborhood and not a commune!

Standing next to Joe DiMaggio and Ted Williams at the White House in 1991, President George H. W. Bush is pretty good company as well.
(Used by permission of the LSU Athletic Department)

LEFT: Clowning around in a photo booth with Kym in 1993 shortly after we met.

RIGHT: Posing with Kym in 1998 just before a date to the Melting Pot on a rare off day.

LEFT: Hanging out with Kym in the Turks. Every year we get away for a few days without the kids for our anniversary. After fourteen years of marriage she says she still likes me. I'm blessed!

RIGHT: Posing with Kym on a getaway in December 2003.

CLOCKWISE FROM UPPER LEFT: Posing with the Braves on family day in 1997. Kym is expecting Colby; Grayson taking a swing at Veterans Stadium in 2000. I think he missed; the always charming Colby Byrd; Kym and Grayson at a spring training game at the old Jack Russell Stadium in 1999.

LEFT: Grayson and Colby riding on Kym's grandfather Wallace Sim Yip. Her grandmother Lilly is supporting Colby. Wallace stormed the beaches of Normandy and received two Purple Hearts.

ABOVE: Grayson giving me a hug just before I pitched on family day with the Phillies in 2000.

RIGHT: Grayson and Colby Byrd at the Little Gym in 2002.

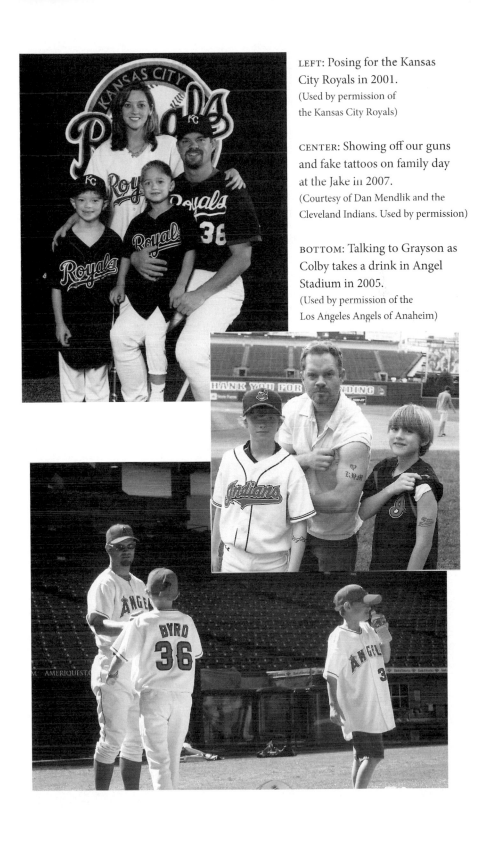

LEFT: Posing for the Kansas City Royals in 2001.
(Used by permission of the Kansas City Royals)

CENTER: Showing off our guns and fake tattoos on family day at the Jake in 2007.
(Courtesy of Dan Mendlik and the Cleveland Indians. Used by permission)

BOTTOM: Talking to Grayson as Colby takes a drink in Angel Stadium in 2005.
(Used by permission of the Los Angeles Angels of Anaheim)

LEFT: Kym's parents, Wally and Mary, in front of the Christmas tree in 2007. Kym is a nice blend of the both of them.
RIGHT: My mom and Larry the Legend at a game I pitched.

At my sister Carletta's farm in late 2000. My two brothers, Mike and Rick, joined us. Mike, with the beard, died on New Year's Day 2001. That was one of the toughest years of my life.

LEFT: This book is dedicated to Kymberlee Byrd.

RIGHT: Kym sitting on a stroller at Disney World during the tired years. Our two boys were wild and we often played man-to-man defense.

LEFT: My smokin' hot life coach. I definitely outpunted my coverage.

LEFT: Colby's friend Jane with her dad, Ben Ortlip, who first read some of my chapters and said I should write a book.

RIGHT: Our friends Wayne, Grace, Trent, Witt, Brant, and Jennifer Waddell. God blessed them with another girl eleven years after the death of their first daughter, Ashleigh Krin.

LEFT: Standing with the Friedmann family after our famous dinner together. Kym is to my left followed by Janet, Morgan, Avery, Frank, Lesleigh, and gentle Ben. Frank has been a great coach and mentor over the years.

RIGHT: The Cagle family, dear friends. Clay, standing next to Janie, died three days later. Tim is holding Gracie.

ABOVE: Speaking at an FCA meeting before Dave Dravecky in 1995.

RIGHT: Doing some kids ministry with a group called LifeSavers.

BELOW: Colby Byrd helping some kids. He has a great heart.

Standing with Mike Lieberthal and Curt Schilling
after making the All-Star team in 1999. Curt and I
were on the bottom of a pile about a month later.
(Used by permission of the Philadelphia Phillies)

My first game back after Tommy John surgery.
Oddly enough I threw to Eddie Perez and beat the Indians.
(Used by permission of the Atlanta Braves)

I was one strike away from a no-hitter against the Mariners
when the game was called due to snow. The next day I was
sledding down a hill in Cleveland with my two boys.
(Used by permission of the Cleveland Indians)

Garret Anderson is one of my good friends in baseball.
Like Mike Sweeney, we have great talks about the goodness of God.
(Used by permission of the Los Angeles Angels of Anaheim)

Winding up with the Indians for
the second time has been a great blessing.

(Courtesy of John Kuntz. Used by permission of the Cleveland Indians)

I grew up in Louisville, Kentucky, home of the Louisville
Slugger Museum & Factory, which has a 34-ton,
120-foot-tall replica of one of Babe Ruth's bats.

(Courtesy of Chuck Schupp. Used by permission)

8

THE MAGNIFICENT PERFORMANCE OF COLBY BYRD

WORKING PRIMARILY through my family and sports, God has taught me that true Christianity is more about being than doing. It is so much more about being accepted, being liked by God even though you come with all sorts of baggage. You are welcomed into a family as a kid through a profound, yet simple childlike faith. It's an invitation that does not come based on your own performance.

The problem for me, however, is that most everything and everyone else in this life has taught me just the opposite, telling me that my physical earthly performance matters when it comes to being accepted. Growing up, if I brought home an A on my report card, I felt approved by my dad. And if I brought home an F, I didn't feel accepted. My coaches got upset with me when I made an error and praised me when I made the play. When I watched the *People's Court*, Judge Wapner tried to give people what he felt they deserved at their time of monetary sentencing. He never gave the plaintiff or defendant a reward for bad behavior.

Another problem that made it hard for me to receive freedom from working my way to God is that I am a doer and if I can't seem to complete something I want to accomplish, I just try harder and harder until I get the job done or collapse from exhaustion. I find myself identifying with Vince Lombardi, the great NFL football coach, who once said, "I firmly believe that any man's finest hour—his greatest fulfillment of all that he holds dear—is that moment when he has worked his heart out in a good cause and lies exhausted on the field of battle—victorious."[1] When it comes to heaven, that kind of theology feels better to me and makes more sense. Strangely, if I'm honest, I think I want to have some part in getting myself to heaven. I don't want to believe and trust. I want to work for it and receive a place next to God for my effort. Something about receiving makes me feel weak. And I hate feeling weak! Sometimes I wish I could work my way to God! I don't want to be a freeloader! Listen to me!

I've spent much of my life bathing in the problem of comparison and working toward being a good person apart from God. Growing up in Louisville, I would judge myself against other people whom I somehow came to the conclusion were better or worse than I was without having all the information that I needed to make that judgment. Even before I received the truth, I used to look at other Christians and wait for them to make a mistake so I could feel better about myself for not having asked Jesus to be the panacea for my sin and to be my sustaining life giver.

I suppose I thought this way and had all of these problems because several thousand years ago my Greatest-Grandfather Adam ate from a tree that God forbid him to eat from. It was the Tree of

Knowledge and its fruit opened his and my eyes to good and evil. Because the option of goodness was revealed out of that devastating bite, I think I grew up thinking that I could be behaviorally and emotionally good enough to be in the private quarters of God. I had only to care enough and put forth a valiant effort. It made me angry to hear Christians say that I couldn't be good enough to qualify for the presence of God. So when someone presented me with the gospel, a second chance at listening to God and re-eating from the Tree of Life who is really Jesus, it sounded like a cop-out. No one gets something for nothing and that is what faith sounded like to me at first. Nothing. The gospel also, at first glance, made God out to be some sort of egomaniac who was on a power trip to display his my-way-or-the-highway plan for salvation.

I continued to reason with myself that nice people who visit nursing homes and who work in soup kitchens don't deserve to live separated from the Lamb of God so I made sure a few of these caring activities were placed on my calendar. I went to a large brick church and mixed in a few rehearsed and repetitious prayers like the Our Father without reading the sentences in the Bible just before that prayer where Jesus tells us to avoid the legalistic memorized replication thinking that God will hear because of the many words. I wouldn't tell my wife the same thing over and over or talk to her with the protocol I used that day at the White House when I shook hands with President Bush, but I equated relationship with God as obtained by simply doing good things and addressing him over and over. Disgusting! God deserved so much better than I was.

There are times even now when I feel that God deserves so much better than my representation of him. Instead of letting God spill out my spirit, I seem to block him. I'm reminded of a few years back when I got to pitch a Triple-A game in Louisville. I had just lost my brother Mike to cancer and instead of enjoying time with my other brother Rick, I got into a shouting match with him as he drove me to the park to pitch. I was so mad and really didn't want to hear what he had to say; I just wanted him to hear my words, which I thought were right, in a surround-sound format. I made sure I got in the last word as I slammed the door shut behind me when I got out of the car. My strategy worked. I got in the last word for almost two years. Although we eventually reconciled, I still get a feeling in the pit of my stomach when I think of that time in my life and the fight I had with my brother. I hate it when there's a great divide in relationships, especially between family members.

Speaking of family members, when Colby Joshua Byrd came into the world in November 1997, I was so proud. My second son made his appearance in a most unique way. Whereas Grayson was covered in blood, Colby came out relatively clean with his face almost spotless. He didn't cry. And he showed no signs of recognizing my voice. He just kind of hung out until a white-coated doctor wearing brown cowboy boots lightly spanked him and made him work his lungs. His legs resembled small sticks and I was afraid to change his diaper for fear of pulling one of his bones out of the socket. Mike McCoy, a close friend of mine with ginormous hands, could literally hold him with four fingers. Strikingly handsome, no one could tell what member of the family Colby resembled; we just knew it wasn't me. I loved that boy, and barring a miracle, he has proved to be my last biological son.

The funny thing is he has turned out to have a disposition that is exactly opposite of the one he displayed at birth. He is loud, aggressive, energetic, and sometimes downright hilarious. He must question me about a thousand times a day. Obviously not hungry in the womb, he has made up for it many times by cleaning his plate and his legs are now big and muscular. Go figure.

When he was a young boy, I finally convinced Colby to brush his teeth by explaining to him that they would eventually fall out if he didn't take care of them. I thought I did a good job until two days later when he promptly told an older checkout lady at Target who had many missing teeth, "We brush ours!" He said this emphatically and with great volume while tapping his upper incisors with little fingers. Many heads from other check-out lanes turned to observe the situation. Kym couldn't lift her eyes from the glossy tiled floor and I almost felt like pushing the half-full cart out of the store without paying. I was mortified.

After a few moments of awkwardness, the very gracious lady said in a soft tone, "I know, baby. I know." I nodded my head at her in a thankful manner with a gentle smile. Her brown eyes accepted my apology and she smiled back at me with a closed mouth.

GRACE AGAIN!

Even though I deeply love Colby, I don't always relate to him very well. Like the time my brother Rick and I had trouble connecting, Colby and I have had many moments of verbal fighting. Whereas Grayson and I "get" each other, Colby and I often end up at opposite ends of the spectrum not understanding a thing the other one is saying. We experience miscommunication so much of the time. If I say to Grayson, "Hey, bud, let's get on your homework," he understands what I am saying and for the most part gets on his homework.

But if I say the same sentence to Colby he usually hears something different than I mean and has often replied, "Why are you always telling me what to do?" Many times when I have told Colby it's time for bed he has looked up at me and screamed, "You hate me!" And I ask myself, *How did we end up here?* I don't know if he is trying to manipulate me into his staying up longer or if he really thinks I hate him. Anyway, it makes me sad.

And believe me, it's not always him. I am to blame much of the time because I have a problem listening and speaking in quiet tones. Sometimes intensity sneaks into my voice during conflict, and I raise my voice way too loudly at him and I keep trying to make my point or get him to do what I want him to do when I should take a step back and hear his words and digest his point of view. I guess I hate being out of control. Kym is working with me on mirroring him, which simply means to listen and repeat back what he said in a different form. This has helped us tremendously except when I'm mad and I don't have the patience for mirroring. I do need to improve my parenting skills. And I need to stop yelling so much.

Trying to raise Colby has given me such an appreciation for my father. I always heard that I was a tough kid to handle, never sleeping, being overly sensitive, often fist-fighting, and becoming argumentative when corrected. I'm now thankful to my father and mother for hanging in there with me. So, maybe Colby gets some of his stuff from me and we're a whole lot more like each other than I sometimes realize.

Because I am a professional baseball player, I sometimes think that Colby feels I would prefer him or be more pleased with him if he performed better athletically. This too makes me sad. Colby is brilliant in the classroom and makes straight As with ease but at this point in life he is not as coordinated as Grayson and hasn't been blessed with the same physical gifts. He is a year and a half younger and sometimes has to work twice as hard as Grayson to accomplish the same athletic skills. More than once I've told Colby he doesn't have to play competitive sports, but it doesn't seem to matter, he insists on playing. The only reason I thought he should stop in the first place is because I believe that competing in organized sports is truly not in his heart. But then again, maybe his heart simply needs my encouragement and he belongs in sports just as much as any other young boy. Maybe I should listen to what I preach about baseball and connecting through fatherhood while simply playing catch.

The only reason I thought about keeping him off a team was due to the fact that growing up he was always the kid who would spin around about ten times to swish the balancing fluid in his ears in hopes of becoming dizzy or the one who would look skyward to notice a flying airplane that just emerged from a cloud. Honestly, I think enjoying the world in this carefreelike manner is a great approach to life, except when a football is coming your way or a ground ball is quickly approaching and your team is counting on you to make the play. Even now when we play flag football in the backyard with the neighborhood kids, Colby chases after brown chirping crickets instead of running his wide receiver route that was traced on the quarterback's T-shirt and usually ends up on some large rock cupping his hands while one of his teammates yells at him in the hope of reminding him to pay attention. Again, he insists on playing. So now I am working with him to have fun, encouraging him to do his best and trying to teach him to enjoy the game even when he fails. Sometimes he gets there and other times he doesn't. Sometimes he laughs. And like me, sometimes he gets frustrated and wants to punch somebody.

One day Colby asked Kym, "Mom, why does Dad like Grayson better?" It would have been a lot cuter if he didn't mean it. It absolutely broke my heart.

Colby is such a great kid! I keep telling him that I simply love him because he's my son but many times it doesn't seem to matter. He still thinks I like Grayson more because his batting average is higher. One day in California, while we were playing a game of Whiffle Ball at the neighborhood park, I sat him down among his frustration and told him, "Colby, look me in the eyes, son. I don't like Grayson any better than you."

"Well, you sure don't show it! You're always cheering for him and smiling at his games!"

Maybe someday soon my words will take and his apparent wound will start to heal. I've heard that a child's personality is formed at a very young age, which scares me tremendously when I think of Colby. He has a great and fun-loving personality but I don't want him to grow up thinking I am not as pleased with him as I am with his brother. I love both of my boys very much, but I also love them differently and for their own unique personalities. I don't have a favorite but I do get a warm emotional rush when I think of their individual and distinctive habits. I just don't want Colby to try to be Grayson. Or Grayson to try to be Colby. Or either of them to try to be me for that matter. God knows the purposes for which he has created each of us. Maybe I can help each of my sons determine their places in this world.

Unfortunately, I only get to see about one or two of Colby's baseball games each year. They are priceless for me. One day this past year, I had an off day in Cleveland and was able to attend one of his games in Westlake, Ohio. I watched him play third base behind a silver chain-link fence. He kept checking on me to make sure that I was watching him. When he made a play and threw someone out at first, he looked over at me and nodded his head while chomping on a big glob of Big League Chew. I smiled at him and said, "Way to go, man!" He got a sheepish grin at the corner of his mouth, which caused a small dimple to appear below his right cheek.

Later in the game, Colby went in to pitch and I took a video camera out to centerfield and recorded him through the fence. Thankfully, he did so well. But the funny thing was, he literally turned and looked at me after each strike he threw. But he never looked at me when he threw a ball that landed in the dirt or sailed high out of the strike zone. And after he struck out two batters in a row he strutted around the pitcher's mound like a rooster scratching the dirt and tilting his head to the side to look my direction so his eyes could confirm that I was still noticing him and that I'd witnessed his success. I lifted my fist high in the air back at him like some scene out of *Braveheart*. Again, he smiled.

Colby does many things well. Not only is he hilarious, but he also remembers jokes with an uncanny ability for a child his age. He is also a great student and a fantastic writer for someone who has just turned ten. He writes short stories about animals that are amazing. Sometimes his stories have a spiritual truth or hidden message mixed into the paragraphs, which end up teaching me something I have forgotten. I don't know if he does this on purpose or not, I just know that there's often a message. A fast reader, Colby likes to read *Captain Underpants* and other adventure books just before bed, which he devours with regularity. Strikingly handsome and full of wit, Colby has never met a stranger and can charm almost anyone. He is like some beautiful poem! A real work of art!

Probably my favorite thing about Colby is that he loves to talk to God. I think there is some kind of spiritual battle going on with him. He is highly sensitive spiritually, hears things and thinks of questions that most children don't even consider. For years, he wasn't confident that he believed in Jesus. He kept asking me how I knew he believed in Jesus.

At the age of eight, he asked me, "Dad, how do I know that I love Jesus?"

"Because you talk to him, think about him, listen to him, and smile when you feel him."

"Yeah, Dad, I know that," he answered, with rolling eyes. "But how do I know that I don't do all of that because I love you and you taught me that way?"

"Well," I said, totally dumbfounded that a person of his age was even capable of asking such a question. "I don't know. Let me work on that one."

The next day I gave him my best answer, which may not have been good enough. "I guess you don't talk to Harvey, the big invisible rabbit, because you don't believe he is standing next to you and you don't like Brussels sprouts even though I like them, so maybe your talking and listening to Jesus on your own means something."

He looked up and nodded. We connected.

Even though Colby and I have had trouble communicating occasionally, I have always resonated with him from a place deep inside of my soul. Perhaps it is because while growing up, I too felt God looking down on me, and somewhere deep inside my inner spirit, I still wanted his approval. I say this because I was married to the Old Testament Law originally, and my thinking was severely distorted.

Similar to Colby's error-filled belief system that tells him I would like him better if he played baseball at a higher level, I took in the lie that God would love and accept me if I performed for him better in this life by doing good things or deeds that I thought he would do. I kept looking over my shoulder through the spiritual fence that I felt separated us, hoping to see a smile or some physical sign of praise every time I did a good deed. I wanted God's approval but didn't even know it. One part of my heart said that God was good and loved me no matter what and the other part told me that he was a stern judge who had to be approached on his terms, not mine. During the times when I couldn't reconcile how God could have this huge ego I mistakenly imagined him to have, I altered my faith by accusing the scribes or translators of the Bible for having made some kind of literary errors over the years, even making God look as if he were a dogmatic and fundamentally mean person. So I tried to make hell, or a place of separation from God, go away.

But that was then and this is now. And from a place where I sit now, a place of having experienced God's great affection for me, I have had to reconsider. I now see heaven as a relationship with a Person and not simply some feel-good place with baseball fields and delightful sunny beaches. Also, I have started to think of hell as a place of separation from God, the Person who loves all of us more than our minds can imagine. I now think that when Jesus spoke about hell being a place of never-ending fire, part of that fire has to do with not being able to be with someone who loved you so much that he was willing to give up his Son to be with you—almost the painful decision to become an eternal orphan instead of wanting to be with a loving Father.

Although I have often had trouble understanding who God really is and that my acceptance by him is not based on my performance, as well as reconciling concepts like hell, I do think I am starting to grow up and realize more and more about the giving heart behind his rules and regulations of love. There is a great mystery to God and a tremendous freedom in truly knowing that my heavenly Father loves me even when I am not currently feeling his love and acceptance. The primary reason I can say this now is because I have entered a new realm, one where I have gotten a taste of what it means to love a child who has trouble receiving my love. My gratitude for that child is just as great as my love and acceptance of him. Again, I'm talking about my son, Colby Byrd.

9

JACOB WRESTLED GOD;
I WRESTLED EDDIE PEREZ

YEARS AGO, while driving to a family reunion in New Orleans, I stared at a bumper sticker on the car in front of me that read, REAL MEN LOVE JESUS!

As you can probably tell by now, I am all for loving Jesus but what took me by surprise were the first two words on that advertisement, REAL MEN. I thought for a moment. What is a real man? What does a real man look like? What does a real man do? Impregnate women? Hit a baseball? Build something? Write something? It can't be as simple as loving Jesus, can it?

Suddenly, I felt a longing in my heart to understand more about the issue of masculinity from God's perspective. Like Pinocchio, I had always wanted to reflect Gepetto and be a real man but if I was honest with myself I was mostly confused when it came to mixing my masculinity with Christianity. From looking at much of what I knew of the Church, it appeared that I should be on some quest to become a soft-spoken nice guy who drives a minivan and buttons the top button on his shirt, which isn't a bad thing for some but just didn't feel right for me when I tried to play that role.

So we pulled our lime green minivan up to the party that day and hopped out to a mob of excited Chinese relatives. Grayson was about three years old at the time and because they hadn't seen him in almost a year, everyone wanted to pick him up and squeeze his candy red cheeks. Grayson felt cornered. Tears started to well up in the edges of his young eyes and he backed up to the cement curb understanding no one. My little boy, now running out of room, leaned his back against the side of the van, pointed his little index finger and made an extremely powerful statement, one that I will never forget. He said, "Paul Byrd is my dad!"

Everyone laughed because his words sounded a little out of place. The family all knew that I was his father, so there was no reason for him to establish his identity. Nevertheless, his words made them realize that he felt pressured and they backed away to give him some time to adjust. When they did, I smiled from a place deep within the recesses of my soul. In a time of trouble he wanted everyone to know that I was his father. Very cool!

The summer after Grayson pressed back the multitude from New Orleans with an emotional sentence, I pitched a game in Atlanta against John Smoltz and the Braves. I was pitching for the Phillies and my not-so-blazing fastball drilled the batter, Eddie Perez, the Atlanta catcher, squarely in the back. Ouch! Because I had pitched against the Braves five days earlier in Philadelphia and hit Eddie in the same spot, it didn't go over too well with him, his teammates, or the Atlanta fans that could be heard booing from all corners of the stadium.

The next batter was John Smoltz and he hit a grounder to shortstop. Eddie got John and himself immediately called out for making an illegal chop block on the second baseman. The Atlanta manager, Bobby Cox, one of the greatest skippers of all time, came out to argue the play and ended up getting ejected for saying mean things to umpires. The next inning, in an effort to balance the scales of worldy testosterone, John Smoltz retaliated by hitting Alex Arias in the back, which got him put in locker room time-out with Mr. Cox. I soon grabbed a bat and walked up to the plate to hit. Before a pitch was thrown, Eddie Perez shouted a few things at me in Spanish that reminded me of an angry Ricky Ricardo and even though I had a year of collegiate Spanish under my belt, I really didn't understand a word of it and stood there feeling like a baffled Lucy.

After the half minute of belittlement, we ended up going after one another until a wall of players led by Curt Schilling, our team's star pitcher, jumped on top of us. Eddie and I continued wrestling each other as I gasped to find any available air, which by the way, is very hard to come by under about forty players. I will never forget that moment that Curt was right there with me. I don't use his name for reasons of clout, I just think it shocked me because at the time I thought Curt would be the last person on our team to go to battle and risk injury for me. At that point in his life, he didn't claim to know Christ and could be heard loud talking fellow players who felt differently on just about any worldly topic ranging from the science of hitting to pitching to politics to religion to fantasy football to the secret schemes of American generals in World War II. He was also our most talented player and had the most to lose if someone accidentally landed a metal spike on his right arm.

Anyway, we both landed on the bottom of the pile and I appreciated his being there. Strangely, we bonded in those oxygen-deprived moments and as our faces began to turn purple, I turned my head to make my eyes meet the Great Spanish-Talking Warrior in what proved to be a chilling stare-off. I was about to literally pass out when my lungs summoned one last breath and my tongue emphatically pronounced, "Eddie, God is my Dad! . . . And you know he will take care of me!" I wasn't sure why I said those words or even if it was me who said those words. I just know that they exited my mouth and when they did, I remembered Grayson and his time of being cornered at the family reunion. I was fearful and yet angry at the same time.

Almost instantly, the mass of players parted and everyone got up in a manner that was similar to the Israelites and the incident at the Red Sea. I'm not saying I was, but for some reason, I felt like I was on fire. I got up and most of the Braves players were staring at me like I was an alien from some other world. I pulled my Philadelphia Red Socks up to my knees and after a short time we all walked back to our respective dugouts. I threw seven innings that fateful night at Turner Field and won the game.

One of their players allegedly said to a reporter after the game, "I don't care that Paul started a fight, I just wonder why he's always talking about the Lord and calling himself a Christian?"

Days after the win, Schilling confessed to me that the whole thing was weird. "You're telling me?" I said while laughing. "I'm still trying to figure out exactly what happened myself." Weeks later, Curt and I had adjoining seats on a long commercial flight back from California. After our plane got off the runway and entered some gray clouds he looked over at me and asked, "So what's up with the Middle East and all this End of the World stuff?" We had a long conversation about the origin of the fighting in Israel, Christianity, and faith as a whole. I thought it strange the way God opened that door, and for the rest of my time in Philadelphia, Curt and I were able to talk about deep spiritual truths. Eventually he told me that he turned his life over to God.

Years before my scuffle, during the playoffs, a pitcher with the San Francisco Giants gave up a crucial home run to give the other team a win. Like that pitcher, I have been there many times. We all make mistakes but in this particular case the losing pitcher walked off the field with no sign of frustration or care in the world. He further complicated matters when reporters asked him why he showed no emotion. He responded by saying, "It was God's will that I gave up a home run."

Many Christian ballplayers were already labeled as being passive, weak, and uncaring and many skeptics thought of us as being too nice to get hitters out or unable to take someone out at second base to stop the double play. I guess they felt that we didn't want to hurt anyone because we associated ourselves with Jesus, a man portrayed in pictures as being sort of an old-school metrosexual who liked to wear white gowns, sandals, and sit on big rocks with children while cute sheep and dandelions filled the background. Scouts considered us nice men but not real men who had the necessary equipment to get the job done. You know, real men.

So many people, including the player who questioned my faith for fighting with Eddie Perez, seem to be confused on the issue of masculinity from a Christian perspective. I have to admit that at times I have gone through confusion and ended up a little off-track as well, especially when I have turned my eyes to the world.

A wonderful writer named Gordon Dalbey pushed an excellent point in a book titled *Healing the Masculine Soul*. Dalbey asks, "What does my own culture offer as a validation of manhood? The driver's license at sixteen; freedom at eighteen to join the army,

149

attend pornographic movies, and to buy cigarettes and beer. The message is clear: Becoming a man means operating a powerful machine, killing other men, masturbating, destroying your lungs, and getting drunk."

He continues, "We're lost males, all of us, cast adrift from the community of men, cut off from our masculine heritage—abandoned to machines, organizations, fantasies, drugs . . . Most of us define ourselves by what we do, who we know and what we own."[1]

POWERFUL

Another thing the world offered me as a validation into manhood was cursing and rage. I didn't know it was possible to be strong without being vulgar. Growing up, I thought "real men" had tempers and used profanity to establish themselves apart from children. I say this because before I became a Christian, I used to use the F word as an adjective, a verb, a subject, a pronoun, a preposition, an interjection, and sometimes as an adverb. And once, after giving up five runs in one inning, I used it as a conjunction, which requires tremendous anger and a superkeen mastery of the English language.

I also used to throw my glove and beat up defenseless silver trash cans. After a while, our team switched to the Rubbermaid brand, which I could no longer damage. This nifty move only proved to cause the small rudder in my mouth to launch a barrage of more and louder dirty words, steering me into deeper waters of rage. Because I threw these well-disguised childlike tantrums as a grown man, my teammates and coaches called me a "Gamer!" They said this because they were proud of me. My mouth showed all uniformed personnel who had working eardrums that I was not a wimp and I cared about the game. And caring is good. Still, I didn't know what a real man was from God's perspective.

Even after Jesus spiritually wrestled my inner man and jumped into my heart, I was confused. I stopped acting like a four-year-old who was told he couldn't have a sucker but I was unsure of how to show I cared. For some reason, I confused Christianity with Buddhism and thought good Christian men were unemotional in times of trouble. Like the Giants pitcher who didn't seem to care, I thought I wasn't supposed to be angry or upset about anything. I was supposed to trust God. I reasoned that since I had Christ in my life, I should have it all together or at least fake it and pretend like I did so that other people could see a true witness in the midst of all of the chaos in this world.

So when I had a rough outing, I began to shake my head in simple frustration and walk over to the bench in a peaceful-like fashion only to let out a wheezy sigh like a freshly popped bicycle tire. I felt bottled up. I was still angry on the inside but I knew that everyone on my team was watching me and I didn't want to ruin the reputation of Jesus, which I mistakenly felt was now utterly dependent on my behavior. I wanted to show everyone that I had changed and I wanted them to notice the tranquility that was supposed to be flowing out of me like a gentle river. So even though I felt like Hulk Hogan on the inside, I looked like Mr. Rogers on the outside and I believed that it was only a matter of time before my top blew and I got kicked out of the Christian neighborhood and my fellow teammates were given permission, in their minds, to refuse Jesus because they noticed I was just like them. To be honest, I felt spiritually castrated! Again, I was confused.

But after a while God began to teach me and I learned that it was okay to love Jesus and be angry and even blow it sometimes. It was okay to pitch inside and play with intensity and show frustration. I found out that it was a much better witness to be passionate about something and show it, accepting the risk that you might mess up or be too intense than it was to simply be sort of a baseball pacifist who acted like nothing could faze him.

Having wrestled with integrating masculinity and Christianity for several years, I had already begun to form my own convictions when I read a book by John Eldredge called *Wild at Heart*. The author was further along on his journey into masculinity than I was and I really appreciated his counsel within the pages. There was a chapter in that book called "The Wild One Whose Image We Bear." It was fantastic! God used that book to help teach me that real men, like God, can have strong emotions and display passion. I continued to learn that my heavenly Father actually desires for me to have emotions, experience desire, joy, pleasure, and pain. It was a great read.

I remember reading in the Bible where God actually commands me to feel, telling me to, "be angry." The difference I think is that he wants me to be holy in my anger and resist sin, which often becomes very tricky for me. I think that's why he follows with the words, "In your anger do not sin" (Ephesians 4:26 NIV).

JESUS. PROPER ANGER

Jesus, the One who showed up as a perfect Man and model for my emotions, cleaned house with a whip, passionately rebuked the Pharisees, turned the other cheek, fervently cared for people, called Herod a name, wept, laughed, and dripped blood from his brow, hugged leprous humans who were contagious, handled women gently with love and respect, changed water to wine for a party, graciously and silently walked over to be slaughtered like a lamb, and yet will come back someday soon with a sword in his hand to take names like a roaring lion. And he is doing all of this because he loves his Father and loves us.

JESUS, THE PERFECT MAN!

All of a sudden these newfound lessons in well-placed emotion allowed me to feel masculine and not so stifled. I thought I might belong in the Christian neighborhood after all and could now be the person that God created me to be, a man who walks with his Father in balance trusting him to shape and complete me as a masculine emotional athletic being. Although I still made mistakes after that realization and didn't always handle my emotions properly, I relaxed knowing that I was still a work in progress and that God would be carrying on until completion. I began to grow and, with God's assistance, slow down the episodes of rage or moments in my life when I lost emotional control. I started to show passion and properly get upset with the disappointing things in my life without quoting a verse about God working all things out to the good of those who love him or sitting down on the bench without looking upset if I had failed. Power under control felt manly.

One of my favorite chapel leaders over the years is a man named Donnie. He does the chapel services for the home and visiting clubhouses at the Oakland Athletics Coliseum. Since Donnie looks like he could be a member of the Raiders defensive line, he fits right in athletically as he shares Jesus with all of us in the back corner of the weight room. Not only does he sport a ginormous body frame but he wears cowboy boots and has thick black hair that he wears slicked back like Pat Riley's. He's intimidating.

Donnie is the director of Radical Reality, a group of modern-day strongmen who do feats of strength before they share some Jesus with the crowd. They have spoken to more than five million young people in public schools over the past twenty-five years. My personal favorite was when Donnie would twist a frying pan into a wrapper like he was repackaging a Fruit Roll-up. I say this because it literally looked like this when he finished with it. A Fruit Roll-up. He would then hand it to me, the team skeptic, and I would try to unroll it. After about fifteen seconds or so of trying to manipulate the metal back into form and getting nowhere, I would nod my head in approval to the rest of the guys and Donnie would begin his talk. I felt like his personal sidekick, kind of a poor man's Ed McMahon. Another feat that I enjoyed was watching him tear the San Francisco Yellow Pages in half with his bare hands. I almost went on the disabled list a few times attempting to do the same thing back at my hotel. I learned that I am not as strong as Donnie and a lot of businesses in Oakland have their numbers listed.

Donnie told me a story one time with tears in his eyes about his earthly father who was dying. It really meant a lot to me and made me think of what it meant to be a real man.

"Paul, a few months ago I had the privilege to sit with my father during his final days. My father was an honest man. He led with great integrity and never compromised what he stood for. He also fought in World War II and loved God very much. During the last two weeks of his life, he made sure to share Christ with everyone in his family because it was important to him that he sees them all in heaven one day."

Donnie paused. He was getting choked up.

"Man, that's awesome," I said. I thought he was finished and to be quite honest that was more than enough for me to get excited about, but he continued.

"The last day that I was with him we were sitting together and I looked over at him and our eyes met. Instantly, I knew how much he loved me. My father asked me to help him to his feet so I got out of my chair and lifted him up. I asked him where he wanted to go but he told me nowhere. I asked him why he wanted to get up and you know what he told me?"

"No," I said.

"He told me, 'Warriors don't die sitting down.' A few minutes later he died right there in my arms."

After Donnie told me that I was still. I felt like someone hit me with a sledgehammer. I decided at that moment in my life that I wanted to die standing up. I was not only amazed at the fact that his father got out of the chair at the last second but because of the posture of his heart and the stance he took in this world to teach people the love of God. That is what made him a warrior. Donnie's father told and lived the truth, just like that bumper sticker. When I hear stories like the one of Donnie's father, I want to engage in loving my Creator and others like a warrior.

One of the greatest stories I have ever read is in the book of Genesis. It vividly deals with the manhood issue. Jacob, son of Isaac and grandson of Abraham, demanded his older brother Esau's birthright for a bowl of freshly prepared stew. Esau, probably having low blood sugar like me, claimed to be near death from a lack of food and decided that the birthright of the oldest was worth trading in his moment of extreme hunger. Later on, their father Isaac asked Esau to go out into the field and hunt some wild game for his own blessing ceremony. Esau, reneging on the deal with Jacob, left to do as he was told. While he was gone, Jacob teamed up with his mother Rebekah and disguised himself to look and feel like his brother Esau and get the blessing from Isaac who was now nearly blind. Feeling the arms of Jacob and believing they were Esau's, Isaac mistakenly gave the blessings of his oldest son to the younger. And when Esau returned and found out that Jacob had also tricked their father and cheated Esau yet again, he wanted to kill Jacob. Their father, Isaac, was emotionally crushed at the way things went down but refused to change his blessing even at the tears and pleading of Esau. Isaac, being a man of God and a man of his word, said, "Jacob will indeed be blessed." Esau, now waiting for the death of his father so he could kill Jacob, boiled with anger. At the request of Rebekah and in order to save his own life, Jacob left his family and went out into the world, being known as the Deceiver.

Jacob's ways come back to haunt him, however, as his uncle and employer deceives him into marrying both his daughters, which in today's culture sounds a little weird. But the part of the story that I find so powerful is when Jacob decides to return home some twenty years later and sends messengers ahead to notify Esau. They come back and inform him that Esau is approaching with over four hundred men. Jacob, apparently fearful of his brother's revenge and still needing to learn different ways, sends his servants ahead to give Esau some of his animals in sort of a brown-nose-like fashion. Splitting up his wives, Jacob sends them out and waits behind feeling scared and upset.

But that night as he sits alone, possibly feeling like a sissy, Jacob meets a man and starts wrestling with him until daybreak. When the man saw that he could not defeat Jacob, he struck the socket of his hip and dislocated it and then demanded, "Let me go for the dawn is breaking."

The part of the story that makes tears roll down my face is when Jacob apparently realizes who he is wrestling with and holds on to the leg of God and screams, "I will not let you go, unless you bless me." I always cry when I read that part because I can really identify with Jacob. I have always loved my mother dearly and have gotten many of my ways from her. Good ones and not so good ones. But I have needed more. And I have looked for validation from my earthly father, Larry the Legend as well, telling one counselor that all I ever wanted to know is that my dad is proud of me as his son, which is sort of like seeking his blessing. But similar to Jacob, I have felt a void in my soul and needed God to confirm my masculinity apart from my parents. In addition to seeking it through pornography or the fantasy of feeling wanted by a naked woman on television. Apart from standing victorious on the athletic fields of men or the stadium parking lots where kids want my autograph. And apart from having a beautiful wife and two strong boys who look up to me. I have not even been able to find that approval through doing good deeds or focusing on being a good person.

The incredible story of Jacob finishes with the man asking him, "What is your name?"

"Jacob."

"No longer will your name be Jacob," the man told him, "but Israel, because you have fought with God and with men and have prevailed."

So Jacob named the place Peniel, explaining, "Certainly I have seen God face to face and have survived."

Jacob, now confident in his adequacy as a man of God, puts his family behind him and limps out to meet his brother Esau prepared for death. However, Esau rushes to Jacob and embraces him, kissing him in joy as they both weep.

Jacob says, "Now that I have seen your face and you have accepted me, it's as if I have seen the face of God."[2]

I have only found true acceptance and masculinity in the person of Christ Jesus and in a wrestling with God the Father that takes place in both my heart and in my mind. Regardless of my sins, I will not let God go! My fight, this scrapping with God while living in a world that sometimes confuses me, has resulted in a revelation and a freedom that tells me I matter to him and that I am adequate and measure up as a man in his eyes. It is like God humors me much in the same way that I do my two boys when we grappled on the living room floor and I make them feel tough by sometimes letting them overtake me. It's in these moments when I pin him and he whispers to my spirit and tells me that I have what it takes.

I think this spiritual wrestling mat is available to all, even if your earthly father has abandoned you, been too critical of you, or left you to fight alone in this world by emotionally detaching himself from your life. And still available to you, even if you relate to your mother better or get your ways from her. And even if you have had good parents like mine, I still believe with my whole heart that ultimately, you will need to get the sense of your masculinity and feelings of adequacy from God.

I don't want to come across as having all the answers on the subject of Christian masculinity because I don't. The title of this book was originally *The Free Byrd Project*. I wanted people to know that I was unsure of many things and still somewhat of a project. But I am learning. And as far as things I do know, I am certain that regardless of your circumstances, God can heal you and he can heal me and reveal just what it means to be a Christian man in this world that can often confuse us and teach us incorrectly. So as I wrestled with Eddie Perez physically, I encourage all men of all ages to visit the powerful and vast arms of God and wrestle him spiritually in hopes of continuing down the amazing journey of discovering more about your sonship and what it means to be a Christian man.

In the end, Jacob's name was changed to Israel, which came to mean the Prince of God. And now, when I see that bumper sticker that says, REAL MEN LOVE JESUS, I smile. Because I do love Jesus and have wrestled with God like Jacob, I too have become a prince, a child of the king, and a real man.

WHEN BAD THINGS HAPPEN
TO GOOD BASEBALL PLAYERS

DURING ONE OF MY LATER YEARS at St. Xavier, I had to read a book for religion class called, *When Bad Things Happen to Good People*. Harold S. Kushner, the author, said in his first sentence of chapter one, "There is only one question which really matters: Why do bad things happen to good people?"[1]

I really liked reading Kushner's book. If I understood the book correctly, the pages conveyed the randomness of the bad things that this life spits out at, generally speaking, good people, and that God is a person who hurts right along with his Creation through the trials, but can't change the unpleasant circumstances that come their way. If God could change or take away the problems of Miss Sally Nice, our All-American next-door neighbor, but didn't, it would leave us questioning his goodness and justice toward all of us. Therefore, we must assume that bad occurrences are simply bad luck and pray to God for the strength to endure it. The last page of the last chapter asks us, "Are you capable of forgiving and loving God even when you find out that he is not perfect, even when he has let you down and disappointed you by permitting bad luck and sickness and cruelty in his world, and allowing some of those things to happen to you?"

I thought Kushner's book was profound and well written, but after becoming a Christian, I had to wrestle with the New Testament scriptures telling me that God is perfect, all-trial stopping powerful, extremely just, and very, very good to me. Given his nature as revealed in the Bible, I couldn't understand that for some reason, he still doesn't stop the trials. As usual, I was confused. I loved God and had accepted his Son Jesus, but other people, including the ones who had not received him, seemed to pass me by on the worldly list of having good things happen to them.

So I rationalized that since I still had some sins in my life, I was getting what I deserved when I got demoted after a season of pitching well or I worked hard and still had tremendous arm pain. After all, there is only One Person who is truly good. However, even as I was trying to make sense out of cause and effect in the Christian life, I noticed that other Christians who were failing far worse than I were getting circumstantially blessed beyond measure, which served only to further confuse me. While playing in the minors, another Christian player I knew was attending baseball chapel and at the same time was having multiple sexual affairs on the road, coming home to a beautiful family, and dominating on the baseball field, which soon got him called up to the big leagues. Here I was trying to walk with God, but instead I kept walking hitters while watching other players who didn't work as hard or seem to care about God pass me by. Although I wasn't perfect, my mistakes or sins seemed to me to be less harmful than the ones my teammate was committing. Not only did I find myself rewarded with an aching shoulder and a damaged elbow, I was married to a beautiful woman who didn't particularly enjoy the baseball lifestyle and times of major separation on the road. Even at home I seemed always to be going to the ballpark, which put a strain on our marriage and left her feeling a little down on my priority list. I was also experiencing clouds of loneliness, insomnia, financial struggles, and severe hair loss. When people that I felt didn't deserve to be blessed seemed to be doing a lot better than I was, I found myself sarcastically asking God, "Are you sure you're running this place, or was Kushner right after all?" Although I'm quite sure that God smiled, I was kind of serious!

God started to answer my sarcastic prayer one night in Baton Rouge while eating dinner with Counselor Frank's family at Roman's Restaurant. Roman's serves Greek food and as we were eating delicious lamb, Frank asked me, "Paul, do you know what sinning is like after we come to know Christ?"

"No," I said.

"It's like tasting this delicious lamb and then after a few minutes, getting up from the table and walking outside to go eat trash from the Dumpster."

Frank's comment hit me hard. I thought of the revolting things that were in large green trash cans and I wondered if I were to ever actually encounter a person eating smelly and stale meat out of one of them, if I would have pity on them or think of them as getting away with something. Obviously, I would feel compassion, and possibly some revulsion, too. But God reminded me that I had looked upon my fellow baseball player, the one who was cheating on his wife, as getting away with something I apparently perceived as desirable. Frank was right. The player wasn't getting away with anything; he was damaging his marriage. I knew the first taste of sin could be pleasant to the palate but I had enough experience in tasting various evils to know that it would soon become bitter to my stomach and circumstantially painful.

I guess Satan never tempts us with the consequences, only the pleasing first bite of sin. The problem wasn't my hypocritical acting teammate, the problem was me, and I needed to change. My view of sin, blessings, rewards, motives, and struggles needed to change. I needed God to teach me.

I started to reconsider my beliefs and, without any sarcasm, I asked God to reveal my erroneous thinking about the blessings and struggles of this world and what he had to do with it all anyway. I found out that becoming angry at God for not always blessing me circumstantially was more about me not trusting in his goodness rather than anything else. Furthermore, I had to come to terms with a growing sense of entitlement, as if God owed me something in the first place. I came to see that I was often focusing on the temporal, rather than the eternal as I pouted when things weren't to my liking. But I gradually began to realize that if I know God is good, all-powerful, and really *for* me, what else matters? In my opinion, embracing those truths about him is far more important than understanding why I have the struggles to begin with. Also, who is to say what a blessing is anyway? If it really is money, fame, health, friends, and getting under the covers with a beautiful wife after a romantic date, then everyone in Hollywood should be fulfilled and the trustworthy tabloids tell me while I'm in the checkout line, that isn't always the case. Maybe the real blessing is in the trial.

All of a sudden, I started to see purpose in the arm pain, the financial struggles, the family troubles, and the fight to stay sexually pure with my eyes on road trips. I guess the first thing my change in attitude did was to reveal how my motives in seeking God had been corrupted from what they were when I first came to believe in him. I mean if the by-product of true Christianity consisted of everything going our way, who wouldn't sign up? Somehow my effort to avoid problems and pain had became more important than loving God and running to him on a daily basis as I faced any number and type of trials.

But I have to be honest and tell you that at times, it still confuses me when things seem to go our way even when we sin. It's equally frustrating when we walk with him and love him and something horrible happens. I just have to remind myself what the truth of the matter is, which goes something like "God is good and I'm not him." Although God knows the pureness of our hearts, along with the motives behind our actions, many times we don't, and I've come to believe there is great benefit when we know if we truly love him or a better lifestyle, like the one I mentioned in chapter three.

So I started to have compassion for my teammate who was leading a double life and genuinely pray for him, asking God to break him of his delusions of worldly satisfaction. Instead of getting angry with the man who was rummaging through the trash, I changed my mind and wanted him to come home and have a prodigal son experience. Instead of being offended by God's grace, I began to offer it up right along with him, wanting to talk to my teammate out of care and not as a finger pointer. I also released my envy and the apparent part of me that still felt sin had something good to offer and turned my eyes back to God.

I think that's one of my problems with the "prosperity gospel" that is taught in some churches today. I recently sat in the large service of a dynamic speaker. The man gave a great talk but at the end he asked everyone to break out their checkbooks and write away. He said that God would bless in direct proportion to the amount that was given. "You have to give if you want to receive!" he said with a thundering voice. I wanted to throw up. Again, I sat back in my chair and thought about motives. I wondered if I could give knowing that a major calamity was about to overtake me. I wondered if I could give simply because I loved. Or if I could give like Jesus who had joy in giving his very life for the guard who jabbed a spear in his side to make sure that he was dead! I would definitely have to rely on God to write numbers in my checkbook on that one.

DEPENDENCE

The Bible verse that I hear quoted the most often goes something like, "Don't worry, brother, God will never give you more than you can handle." I hear well-meaning people say it with a big smile on their face, their countenances looking somewhat like Alfred E. Newman's, the freckled kid who appears on the cover of *Mad Magazine*. And they use that phrase like the ace of spades or some trump card that ends a card game. I want to slap them. There's just one problem with that Scripture verse. It's not in the Bible! Try throwing that verse at a family that has just lost their child or a single mother who has just been diagnosed with cancer. I do know that God provides a way out for us when we are tempted but I often think he allows us to be overloaded with problems in this life so that we can run to him. In other words, God definitely gives or allows us to receive more than we can handle on this earth. The truth of the matter is that we cannot properly handle anything apart from God! Not even the trials of success. And that is another reason bad things happen to good baseball players, so we can look to him.

As the Apostle Paul said, "We do not want you to be uninformed, brothers, about the hardships we suffered in the province of Asia. We were under great pressure, far beyond our ability to endure, so that we despaired even of life. Indeed, in our hearts we felt the sentence of death. But this happened that we might not rely on ourselves but on God, who raises the dead" (2 Corinthians 1:8–9 NIV).

Steve Moultrie, a car dealer from Alabama, told me an interesting story one time about trials.

"Paul, did I ever tell you the story about the older lady in my congregation who fed squirrels?" he asked with a thick Southern accent.

"No, I haven't heard that one," I responded, thinking to myself, *What can a person possibly learn spiritually from squirrels?*

Steve continued, "This woman began to feed these squirrels in her backyard. She would sit out on a picnic table and hit the nuts on the wood and lay them on the bench. A couple of months went by and the squirrels began to trust the lady and depend on her for their food. She opened the screen door on her porch and started tapping the nuts on the ground to get them to come and eat closer to the house. Gradually they did. One day she closed the screen door while they were eating on the porch because she didn't want the squirrels to face any danger from the outside world like dogs or kids with Red Ryder BB guns. The older lady began to develop such affection for the little creatures that she began to feed them shelled pecans and cashews from a jar of Planters Mixed Nuts. The squirrels were in squirrel heaven as they lounged around all day getting fat and becoming slow of foot, free from struggles. They trusted the lady so much that they even began to let her pet them. Do you know what happened soon after?"

I thought for a moment, "No, I don't, Steve, but how can I get one of those squirrels for my kids? They would be great for show and tell."

"You can't," Steve answered.

"Why not?"

"Because they're all dead."

"Dead?"

"Yes," Steve said. "She killed them."

"Killed them?" I asked. "Like in a horror film?"

"No," he responded with a chuckle. "They all died because their teeth grew too long. When they didn't have to crack any of the nuts their teeth never got filed down and the next thing you know they had grown so far out of their mouth that the ends of them began to curl below their bottom jaw. They were grotesque looking, couldn't chew anything, and soon after were skinny and dead."

"Hmmm . . ." I said.

I have read in parenting books that studies show overprotection or sheltering your children can have the same damaging effects on a child's development as constant physical or verbal abuse. One therapist I know from Atlanta believes that overprotecting children is the worst form of abuse. By the looks of this world, I am quite sure God is not into overprotection. I guess I should take heart that his Son has overcome the world. I give thanks that he is shaping me for his eternal purposes through the trials I continue to face. And I am grateful that my teeth haven't grown so long I can no longer crack open the nuts he has provided.

I am not saying that I haven't enjoyed the blessings and good things that have come my way over the years. It just bothers me that from time to time I have focused too much on the good things and bad things that happen in my life as I attempt to walk with God. I realize that I continue to try to determine if there is any correlation between my behavior and the blessings I continue to enjoy. I have to confess that sometimes I still catch myself trying to manipulate God so that I can avoid as much pain as possible.

Speaking of pain and bad things, shortly after the end of the last millennium, I paid off the mortgage on our house and I still had over a million dollars left. Because I had done so well in the late nineties trading Internet stocks, I continued to do so after I had a large nest egg. I mean if you have one million in the bank why not make it two? So I bought stocks on margin and promptly lost all we had saved up. The Internet bubble had burst. All of a sudden, I understood why people jumped off tall buildings when the stock market fell during the great depression. I might've considered that but I would have been unable to get to the roof of our house because my arm was in a sling. It was in a sling because I had major shoulder surgery, a sizable labrum operation that few pitchers ever recovered from.

So there I sat with little hope that I would ever throw again competitively. Instead, I spent my days working out a strategy with the federal government to get on a payment plan to pay taxes. I was very embarrassed when I had to tell my wife that we had to take out a loan on our house, which was already paid off. My brother Mike also lost a battle to cancer, which hurt terribly and triggered an avalanche of family dynamics that caused even more pain. Because my arm was hurt, I had no job. My lifelong battle with insomnia shifted into a new gear and I was miserable. I figured that this was the stuff breakdowns were made of, so I promptly had one. I don't know if it was an official breakdown or not, I just know that I couldn't leave my house for five days. I think I was clinically depressed. I never got examined because I was too upset to walk across the driveway and get into my car to go see a doctor so I just diagnosed myself.

During that time, I would only talk to one person outside of my immediate family, a friend named Buddy Patrick who I knew had gone through similar circumstances. He sort of coached me through my murmuring and brokenness. It's amazing who you turn to when things really fall apart. I think it's rarely the most educated, the wisest, the one everyone knows never had a problem, or the one with little humility. It's always the person who has been where you are and has survived. It's the person who is honest and real about themselves and can empathize and listen.

During that time, Counselor Frank left me a humorous phone message that Kym played from the recorder. It said, "Hey Paul. It's Frank. I just want to let you know that the best way to have a nervous breakdown is to try *not* to have one. Okay. Bye."

All in all, that chapter of my life proved to be one of the greatest things that ever happened to me. Like an animal shedding its coat or getting new skin, I had received a new life. It was a gut check and a major test to find out what my life was all about. I learned that accumulating stuff can be dangerous. I had started to depend on money, my right arm, and good things like a loving family to be my safety net without even knowing it. Losing worldly toys and a comfortable residence built of bricks and cement made me return to an earlier gift that was given to me, one that I could not lose. I returned to God who is my Father, my rock, and my refuge. I leaned on him again.

Eventually, I peeped my head outside our house again and smiled. I even healed up physically from surgery and began to make money again. But when I caressed Uncle Sam's currency, it didn't have the same hold that it had on me before. I had bottomed out and came to the end of myself. I don't hate green paper now or use it to start fires. That's not what I'm saying. And I do believe it's okay to have nice things. I was just appreciative for God's financial blessing without making it my life or something I would fall back on anymore.

Strangely, my wife says I am a more honest and real person since that time in our lives, not always having the right scripture answers for her or everyone else's pain. From then on, I was better at listening and identifying with people's pain, understanding that it could have purpose that I was unaware of and when I did give advice it came in a much more gentle fashion.

While I was going through that difficult time in my life, a friend of mine named Tim Cagle was still reeling from the aftershocks of a crisis of his own just a few streets over from me. I know that we are not supposed to compare our burdens with others in this lifetime but I couldn't help thinking that God had allowed a much heavier load on the Cagle family than the one I was enduring. I had to take a deep breath when I heard Tim's story and realize that we are all in different places and have to focus on the fact that God gives us the Grace to handle our own problems and not always the ones of others.

Tim was a hardworking CPA who was happily married to Janie, his high school sweetheart. They also had two children. Their first was named Clay, an eleven-year-old boy who loved to golf and idolized Payne Stewart, even dressing like him when he went to the course. Because he could already shoot lower than his father, it was rumored that Clay was headed for the PGA Tour. Tim laughed one time when three of his friends called the house looking for Clay because they needed a fourth. Tim went to grab his own clubs and join them only to find out that they weren't joking, they really did want his son. Gracie was their other child, a delightful little girl with the thickest brown hair I had ever seen. Gracie was a typical three-year-old, loving to play and laugh and listen to stories. Everybody in the family loved Jesus and loved each other. And it was obvious in every area of their lives. They lived out their faith and lived among the blessings of this world.

However, on September 14, 1999, a month before Payne Stewart died in a chilling plane crash, Clay was running out of his upstairs bedroom to hand Gracie a toy when he started to fall and yelled, "Mom . . . Help me!"

Gracie ran over to Clay who was now lying on his back in the upstairs hallway. Janie and Tim's mother came flying up the stairs to find Clay passed out with a face that was quickly turning purple. Janie had made it all the way through nursing school but at the last minute decided to become a teacher. Now, seeing purpose in her training, Janie was trying to help her son. She had trouble finding a pulse and began to give him CPR. Immediately, Clay started to get the color back in his face. Tim, who was working in the basement office, came running upstairs after Janie opened the downstairs door and yelled, "Clay has fallen!" When Tim got upstairs he called 911 and knelt over Clay in what proved to be the longest minutes of his life. Gracie sat back behind the both of them, shutting her eyes and cupping her ears as she bowed down to the ground.

As Janie tried to breathe life back into her son, she looked up and noticed a crowd of people huddled around Clay all touching him with their hands. Janie says they were angels. She says this because they looked similar to people but had an incredible radiance about them, a light so bright she could barely see.

She turned to Tim and said, "Do you see these people?"

"What are you talking about?" he replied.

Janie tried to get the angels' attention but none of them would look up. They just kept focusing on Clay and seemed oblivious to her attempts to get them to notice her.

"You can't have him!" Janie screamed out with tears bursting from her eyes.

After twenty-two minutes, the ambulance arrived and because Janie wouldn't give up Clay's body, they all started working on him together.

Janie already knew that Clay was gone, saying later, "I gave birth to him. I felt him come into this world. There was a time when I was trying to revive him when I felt his spirit leave. But I couldn't give up. I loved him so much."

For whatever reason, Clay died that afternoon and God allowed it. The doctors suspected a problem with his heart.

Days later, Tim and Janie sat Gracie down to talk to her about Clay's death but when they began to speak they found out that she knew more about the situation than they did.

"I know Clay died," Gracie said. "They took him out of his body and into the shine and took him into the attic. They sing loud."

As it turned out, unlike Tim, Gracie saw the angels too and shut her eyes because of their magnificent light, the power she called the shine. Unlike Janie, Gracie heard them singing loudly and had to cup her ears to protect them. After a few minutes, Gracie looked up and saw them taking her brother upward into the ceiling to a place she knew as the attic. She told Janie, "Mom, Clay was so happy."

Tim and Janie wept and so did I when they told me the story. In the years that followed, they continued to hurt immensely. They know they will see Clay again but there is still tremendous pain in the waiting.

Even though I believe it is okay to ask God why, Tim says that he has never once done so, only asking him for strength and the courage to move on without trying to forget. I don't know why bad things happen to good accountants and their wives and their children. Tim loved Jesus. He still does. The power of the cross some two thousand years ago made his heart good. His wife Janie is one of the most devout prayer warriors I know. Neither I nor anyone else has any answers for them, nor should we have. I just know that I admired their family as they continued to sit in the pain and genuinely smile about God, while recovering from a heartache that will always have some sort of emotional scar. Tim didn't downplay anything, his desire, his pain, his hope, or his love for Jesus. Nor did he deny at times a longing not to feel the pain. The difference I noticed in Tim Cagle and his family is that I saw Jesus among their pain. I saw the Father in a hurting father, a Wonderful Counselor in a tender mother, and a beautiful, child-like faith in a little girl who believed and experienced an incredible taking of her brother.

I am not happy about the death of Tim's son but neither am I about the death of God's. But I know that the kernel had to fall and the death of Jesus had to happen even though I feel pain over having a part in causing it. I have a solemn respect and thankfulness for the purpose of it. It was necessary. Although I don't know the purpose of Clay's passing, I do know that God does and I have come to trust him in my pain and that of others. But it is still not easy.

The Apostle James once wrote to the scattered Jewish Christians, "Consider it pure joy, my brothers, whenever you face trials of many kinds, because you know that the testing of your faith develops perseverance" (James 1:2). Ken Boa is a Bible teacher and writer who lives in Atlanta. He has repeatedly taught his weekly class that we can either interpret God and the Bible by our circumstances, or we can interpret our circumstances by God and the Bible. When any of us face tragedies like the one Clay and his family have survived, that interpretive choice becomes painfully clear. It's only when we view life from God's point of view that any of us can consider the trials as joy.

Now that time has passed, I sit on the board of the Clay Foundation, a nonprofit ministry designed to help kids. Tim and I meet every so often. One night, while eating at Red Lobster, we started talking about Clay again. We talked about whether or not it was better to have loved and lost or never have loved at all. I've heard it debated that if you never love you can avoid hurting and prevent serious pain.

He looked me straight in the eyes and said with a fierce sincerity, almost angrily, "I'm telling you right now, I would do it all over again. No question. It is worth it to have loved. And very deeply!"

We gave each other knuckles. I felt like he just hit a walk-off grand slam or something. It was awesome. I love it when people stand up for God despite his mysterious allowances and accept the inherent risk of pain.

Maybe when my spirit is stretched out in the heavens, if I still care to know, God will explain to me all of the reasons bad things happen to good ballplayers and good accountants but until then I will endeavor to walk in faithfulness and continue to be refined through the trials because I know that God is able to stop any of them, even though he sometimes doesn't. I now have an answer to the question Kushner posed to my heart a long time ago while I studied his pages at St. Xavier. I found freedom in a solution that wasn't given to me in the book. I give it slowly . . . Our Everlasting Father is omnipotent, Jesus has made my spirit clean, I will have trials, and God is very, very good!

GOD IS MY PITCHING COACH

CHARIOTS OF FIRE won best picture in 1981, and although I watched some of it as a teenager, I really didn't understand its powerful message until later on in life. The film is based on a true story about two British track athletes competing during the 1924 Summer Olympics in Paris. One runner was named Harold Abrahams, a Jewish student at Cambridge, and the other Eric Liddell, a Christian missionary who is soon heading off to China.

But the movie is more than a story about men running; it's about why they run and the source of their strength during competition. Abrahams is a driven man, running to prove a point and to gain the respect of his peers while fighting the subtle anti-Semitism of the day. Liddell, the Flying Scotsman, runs from a heart set free to show the glory of God. He tilts his head back, opens his mouth, and flails his arms while racing around the track looking wildly poetic. Compared to Abrahams, a man of pure form, Liddell's style is drastically different.

I think the greatest line in the movie came after Jennie, Eric Liddell's sister, says, "Training, training, training. All I ever hear about is training. Do you believe in what we are doing here or not?"

She continues to pace around the room upset that he doesn't seem to care about going back to China to share the gospel. "Your mind is not with us anymore. It's full of running and starting and medals . . ."

After signing an autograph for a young girl, Eric takes his sister out into a field that overlooks Edinburgh. He notices the view as Jennie pouts while looking at the ground. Eventually, he takes his sister by the hand and makes her look into his eyes, and that's when he says it: "Jennie, I believe that God made me for a purpose, for China, but he also made me fast and when I run, I feel his pleasure! To give it up would be to hold him in contempt. And to win is to honor him."

That message was so powerful for me. Eric Liddell wasn't on any power trip or program to please God, he simply enjoyed running and offered up his lightninglike speed to our Father. If he won, he perceived the medal as a sign of respect toward God. I got the feeling that he cared about God's timing only and seemed to sit at God's feet enjoying him instead of furiously trying to serve him.

That's what I want to be like. I want to pitch, write, and even offer up the simple tasks of the day like doing the dishes to my Father. I want to feel more of his pleasure as I move my arms and legs while letting go of the baseball or walking across the yard to play with my two boys. I want to give my best without fearing failure or getting caught up in what I'm going to be doing next year. I just simply want to exist as a child of God who tilts his head back and finds freedom in thinking only about today and playing or living for an audience of One.

I read a story one time where Liddell was running a race and was dead last. A spectator said to another, "He'll be hard pressed to win this one!" The other replied, "He's fine, he hasn't even tilted his head back yet." About that time, the Flying Scotsman threw his head back, started flailing his arms, and blew past everyone. I smiled when I read those words. I thought of Justin's Jellybean, the horse from Churchill Downs that always stumbled out of the gate and usually managed to come in first.

I have a jar of brown sand in my locker. It's not from any horseracing track or beach where I pretended to run with my head back like the Flying Scotsman. And even though some people think I use it for cheating or scratching up baseballs before games, it's not for that either. I have never done that although I have been tempted and even fondled a couple of baseballs that have had major scuffs on them.

Wait a minute; I'm lying!

Doctoring a baseball has long been an art form and before I became a Christian, I participated. One summer, I threw baseballs that had K-Y Jelly on them. It was a great pitch for me. It acted like a nasty spitball only it didn't have any saliva on it. I just said that it did because I didn't want anyone to know that I really had a suspicious contraband lubricant stuck behind my right ear. For a while, I justified it by telling myself that the hitter was probably using a corked bat and I was just trying to even up the playing field a little by pulling out a slippery trick of my own. Eventually, I got caught in Riverfront Stadium at a Cincinnati Reds baseball tryout when a scout noticed the catcher kept wiping his hand on his right pant leg after every returned throw. He laughed and the Reds drafted me in the thirteenth round.

Thankfully, I declined their offer and went to college where I met Wayne the Cult Member who led me to Christ. He informed me I was cheating and God loved me so much that he actually cared how I lived my life. At first look, this came across as boring to me and sort of a killjoy. I wanted to use the ever-popular line that goes something like, "Everybody else is doing it," but I didn't. Instead, I just sat there and listened. I guess deep down inside there has always been something very attractive about honesty to me.

Wayne continued by saying, "If you give people enough time to work things out in their heads they can justify most any behavior, even murder." Sometimes I think Wayne's right.

Over the years, I have had many temptations. My specially selected worldly enticements have not just been limited to baseball either. As I've mentioned in previous chapters, they seem to run across a much larger spectrum.

Anyway, the brown sand is from a demolished field in Haines City, Florida, where I asked God to become my pitching coach back in spring training of 2002. I am aware that telling people I asked God to do such a thing brands me as a religious nut, but I also know that when writing a book, lying can get you sued so I figured I had better tell the truth on all accounts.

COMING CLEAN

I was playing for the Royals that year and trying to come back from shoulder surgery. My velocity had dropped severely due to the extensive trauma my upper arm experienced at the hands of a highly skilled doctor, a sharp knife, and some thread. My shoulder, or the round fleshy socket that connects my arm to my body, felt like it had a piece of glass stuck in it every time I threw the ball. And that was *after* the surgery. Because of the pain, I had a feeling that my time in baseball was coming to an end.

After everyone left for the day, I walked out to the many pitching mounds that were near the back of the Boardwalk and Baseball Complex, the site for the Royals spring training. This was the place where earlier in the day most minor league pitchers all worked simultaneously, hoping to get noticed and separate themselves from the numbers of talented players. I prayed. I started off my conversation by thanking God for the time he had allowed me to pitch in professional baseball knowing that many people had never even made it to the mounds where I was sitting. I felt privileged. Even though I was in pain and going through another trial, I felt blessed.

I said, "Father, thank you for crafting my paths to play at this level. I mean it. I don't know what you have in store for me this year but if I can have any say in it, I want to stay in baseball. You know the pain that I'm in. I know you're all things to me. I have never asked you this before and I'm not sure why I haven't but I would love for you to be my pitching coach. Maybe you could show me something or bring something to my mind that would help my arm. I'll pitch in pain if you want me to but I would rather not. I'm at a place where I'm not even enjoying throwing the ball. I'm always wondering how bad the next pitch will feel. I really need you right now and I know that I always need you but for some reason I feel desperate. I feel like the game is fading away from me. On second thought, can you please take the pain away?"

I listened.

I heard nothing.

I felt nothing.

While holding some sandy dirt in my right hand, I continued to talk to my Dad and God who was quiet that afternoon, gently sprinkling the sand over the white pitching rubber. When I finished my time of talking and listening, I got up and began to work on my pitching mechanics. Even though I was in my street clothes and wearing brown leather sandals, I started imitating the delivery of every pitcher that popped up in my memory bank, whether living or those I remembered from faded highlight reels. I leaned. I started twisting and swinging my arms and doing the windmill like Warren Spahn, the winningest left-hander of all time. Then I kicked my leg up above my head like the powerful Bob Feller, a right-hander with incredible flexibility who brought the heat. I bent over. I pushed. Then I fell. And in an instant, I was reminded why pitchers over the years chose cleats instead of sandals while throwing a baseball. I continued by winding my arms up really fast and then dropping them slowly. I swung them back and forth and hoped God would make the pain in my shoulder go away. I kicked higher and faked a throw to home as if a catcher were there. I exaggerated my arms and legs like a wild man. Again I fell. I got up.

Basically, I looked like a man having a seizure or someone being attacked by a swarm of bees. I knew if anyone was secretly watching me that day, they would have called 911 to report some trespasser or crazy fan having a breakdown in fantasyland. When the smoke cleared, I decided to change my pitching motion. I kept the swinging arms and slight bend in my knees at the start of my windup. I also decided to stay hunched over in the middle of my delivery in hopes of hiding the ball for a split second longer.

I threw batting practice the next day and the hitters laughed at first, but soon after they talked about not being able to see the ball clearly. The pain was still there but I had a little more speed on the ball while putting forth a little less effort. I guess momentum does have its advantages. I also suppose the quietness of God is sometimes very loud and even though he didn't take away my pain as I'd asked, he had come through for me on a different level. A level that I had to take on faith.

After throwing batting practice, George Brett, the man Ted Williams called the greatest clutch hitter of all time, called me over.

"You know, Paul, I would have hated to face you."

"Are you serious?"

"Yeah, very. I always liked guys that threw about ninety-five. You know, straight and hard. That way I could time them. I might miss their first one but after that, look out. But you mix things up. You throw about four different pitches and change speeds on all of them. As a hitter, I hated that."

I couldn't believe that George Brett was saying that he would have hated to face me. Get serious! I knew a lot of average left-handed hitters who loved facing me so it didn't make much sense to my brain that a Hall of Fame hitter of his caliber would have been upset seeing my name penciled in the lineup when in fact I thought he would have jumped for joy and done a cartwheel.

I gained a lot of confidence that day and began to trust God in the pain on the field. And even though I relied on God, I also tried to do everything that was legal and in my power to move forward as well. I think there is a little mystery involved when it comes to working and yet allowing God to operate his life through you to display his power and not your own. Somewhat of a togetherness.

I had a great summer for the Royals, winning pitcher of the year for the organization. Even though my fastball still came out slowly, swinging my arms before the pitch helped me throw harder and delay the hitter from picking up the ball. After a time, it became my trademark.

Years later, I made a special trip, returning to the site of those mounds at the Boardwalk and Baseball Complex but they were gone. I think it was being demolished to make way for some condominiums and nice Florida town homes. So I went to the general area where I prayed and grabbed some dirty sand. I felt like Jacob when he returned to set up stones at Peniel, the place where he wrestled with God. In my own sort of unusual way, I had done my own wrestling with God on that sunny afternoon and asked him to stay in baseball and compete with men.

I think I gained some masculinity on that pitching mound, becoming more of a true man. Instead of being a deceiver and choosing to start cheating again, I walked forward and threw with a limp in my shoulder. The pain became a reminder of my dependence. I think God honored that experience and enjoyed our wrestling. There were also innings that season when I felt like the Flying Scotsman, pitching like a strange person, swinging his arms and legs for the glory of God. I know my fastball wasn't the fastest and there were many times when I lost that year but even in those frustrating moments while walking off the field, I really think I felt God's smile run across my heart.

Counselor Frank once told me that Jesus never did anything on his own while walking in this world. He quoted a verse from the second chapter of Acts when Peter, a Jewish man, addressed many of his people. He said, "Men of Israel, listen to this: Jesus of Nazareth was a man accredited by God to you by miracles, wonders and signs, which God did among you through him, as you yourselves know" (verse 22 NIV). Peter continued to explain to the people how Jesus had fulfilled the prophecy spoken through David that noted the Messiah's body would not see decay.

But the part that Frank made me aware of was the fact that God the Father did these things through Jesus, his Son. It doesn't say, "Jesus did them separately." All of a sudden, I began to read in other places where Jesus sounded like a young boy to me in some adult-looking jar of clay or grown-up body. As a man Jesus said, "My Father is always at his work to this very day, and I, too, am working" (John 5:17 NIV).

When the people started harassing him, like they do me in large stadiums when I don't do what they want me to do, Jesus gave them this answer: "I tell you the truth, the Son can do nothing by himself; he can do only what he sees his Father doing, because whatever the Father does the Son also does. For the Father loves the Son and shows him all he does. Yes, to your amazement he will show him even greater things than these. For just as the Father raises the dead and gives them life, even so the Son gives life to whom he is pleased to give it. Moreover, the Father judges no one, but has entrusted all judgment to the Son, that all may honor the Son just as they honor the Father. He who does not honor the Son does not honor the Father, who sent him" (John 17:19–23 NIV).

So it began with me, a spiritual revelation that Jesus operated by the power of the Holy Spirit and was deeply connected to his Father. I learned that the same God and Father who enabled Jesus now lived inside of me and I now felt his pleasure when I walked off the field even if I was upset and, in a worldly sense, had failed. I still showed emotion but I had more of an inward dependence on God to do things with me and through me like Jesus.

I almost accused Counselor Frank of blasphemy one time. He borrowed a quote from Jesus and said, "He who has seen me has seen the Father."

"Yeah, I know that verse," I said like Captain Scripture Answer Man.

"No. I am not talking about Jesus, I am talking about me."

As I pulled my cape over my shoulder and began to back up he began to laugh.

"Relax, Paul. What I mean is that if God worked through Jesus and we can do nothing apart from Jesus, then we must get our source of life from him. In other words, we connect into Jesus who is still connected into the Father so it all goes back to him. When we ignore our flesh and walk by the Spirit, we are really displaying the power of God the Father. This changed life comes through when we love somebody from him and with him. So in truth, if you have seen me in the moments when I have walked with God and noticed my caring heart, you have really seen the Father."

POWERFUL

One of the most intriguing people to me who relied on God was a man named Nicolas Herman. At eighteen, he received a revelation into the providence and power of God that changed his life source. Later, denying the world, he changed his name to Brother Lawrence and joined the Carmelite Monastery, which was a group of lay brothers who sought to devote themselves to prayer. I read a book called *The Practice of the Presence of God*, which was amazing. Brother Lawrence had such a fantastic view of the world and his earthly calling and in those pages I could tell, like the Flying Scotsman, he had sold out to loving God.

But the most amazing thing that overtook me in that book was the fact that as the great and all-powerful God began to live his life through Brother Lawrence, he felt the need to serve and wash the other brothers' dishes. I was expecting him to make some thunderous announcement from atop a mountain or call fire down from heaven to destroy an earthen city that had a special liking for evil. But no, the power of God led him to serve. With God as his strength, he offered up the mundane tasks and doing the household chores no one else wanted to do and gave glory to his Father for the strength to do them. He began to talk and listen to God constantly as he went about his work becoming an amazing witness into the Power of God before everyone who passed.

I do not know if Nicolas Herman took the name Lawrence of the Resurrection knowing the power of the risen Christ would work through him and teach him and others what true strength is. I only know that God did work through Brother Lawrence and his conscious awareness of God became contagious to so many. Seeking people down through the centuries have gained more of an understanding of what it means to walk and talk to God while relying on a strength that comes from the Almighty because of his life and example that started in a small kitchen.

Maybe that's what it is for me. In reality, I throw a ball past a guy who holds a stick. And at times, I don't even do that well. But a greater reality is that I try to rely on the power of God to work through me whether I am cleaning the dishes or pitching in some stadium that is full of thousands of people. I have to constantly remind myself that it is not what I do that matters as much as who I do it from that counts. I don't want to live *for* God; I want to live *from* him. In that way, as Counselor Frank indicated, when you see me walking with God you can say you have seen something of the Father and his power. And by the way, he's not only a great Pitching Coach, he is the source of life for everything else that concerns us, too.

MIKE SWEENEY
AND THE HOUSE OF GOD

MY WIFE KYM is a smokin' hot, certified life coach who loves Jesus. She administered a spiritual personality test to me one time on a green canvassed couch in Cleveland. I failed. I came back as a postmodern fundamentalist, which is kind of like ordering a large pizza with everything on it and a Diet Coke. She laughed and called me a big oxymoron. I told her it isn't nice to call people names. Whatever.

Minutes later, I snuck off to the laundry room and went online to Wikipedia, the free Internet encyclopedia, in hopes of reevaluating myself and finding out more about what those terms meant. I needed clarity. And if I did have some sort of spiritual multiple personality disorder, I wanted to get help.

As best I could tell from researching the terms on my computer, postmodernism had too many definitions for me to understand and apparently meant many different things to many different people, including Christians. I do know that I am into feelings, experiencing God on a deeper level, and a personal and radical reappraisal of true Christianity when it gets confused as a system of mundane rules and lifeless regulations. So if that's your definition of a postmodernist, sign me up. I am one.

I researched the word fundamentalism and found out that it had different definitions as well. I do think the Bible should be taken literally but also I think the absolute truth of scripture should be interpreted correctly. Granted, that can be tough, especially if you're not God or have trouble discerning and listening to the Holy Spirit. Therefore, I try to give grace to other people and myself, when we haven't arrived and fathomed all the mysteries of God since the creation of the world. I do, however, believe that there are universal truths that are available to those who earnestly listen to God after he knocks on the door of their heart. Although I will not gouge my eye out if it causes me to sin or slap someone upside the head with a big thick Bible when they feel differently about scripture, I do consider myself a fundamentalist.

As I've written in earlier chapters, I was raised in Catholicism and became a believer during my years of mass, but I began to bathe in other Christian traditions and services after seeing the Light more clearly during my college years. I think I did this because I began to figure out very early in my walk with God that not everyone who sang Christian songs in the buildings first erected by Constantine loved Jesus. I grew increasingly outraged at the thought that church services were filled with people who neither knew nor loved God for about an hour; then the Holy Spirit reminded me I was in the same boat for most of my life. So in an effort to better understand the church of my upbringing, I lived in a Catholic rectory for a few months questioning my friend John Deatrick who was a Catholic priest, and I got even more confused.

I told him I was considering leaving the Catholic Church because they had some doctrines that I no longer agreed with. I had trouble with the infallibility of the pope when he sat in his papal chair and the fact that Mary, the mother of Jesus, was all of a sudden declared sinless after being thought to have had a nature like us for many, many centuries. What if I wanted to become a Catholic priest? Why couldn't I take a smokin' hot wife and have children?

He responded, "Paul, do you consider yourself an American?"

"Yes."

"Do you agree with everything the Unites States stands for and believe in every law the government has established?"

"No."

"Are you considering leaving the country and taking up residence in France because you have trouble with our government allowing abortion?"

"No."

"Well, then, maybe you should consider staying in the Catholic Church and putting up with your differences."

We were playing Ping-Pong at the time and I chucked my paddle at him! He ducked and I missed. I had no idea a Catholic priest could be so fast.

"Well," I said, while picking up my paddle off the ground. "What if a person is going to get married and doesn't believe adultery is wrong or doesn't want to experience life for better or worse with their partner, kind of planning to just coexist. Is that wrong? I mean, shouldn't you believe in or at least try to follow the major tenets of the deal before you say yes?"

"Yes," he said, while chucking his paddle back at me. "I guess you would have to make that decision. You have to decide where

191

that cutoff point is and figure out where you are most comfortable sitting, standing, and kneeling."

So I ventured out into the world and tried different churches, but I found this common spiritual haze existed among most of the members and in almost all formal services whether they were Baptist, Lutheran, Methodist, or a part of other Protestant denominations. I didn't stay very long in any of them, not wanting to exhaust myself on the religious seesaws of doctrine and separation. I became frustrated in my quest when I attended some Pentecostal services, which were confusing for me coming from Catholicism. So I kept looking for the big-building church where all the members loved Jesus and had all of the correct doctrines. Sadly, I kept running into dead ends.

After a while, I ran into a man named Elihu Ben Yacov, who identified himself as a Messianic Jew or a Jewish person who had received Jesus as the Jewish Messiah. This too sounded crazy to me. I had been taught that all Jewish people didn't like Jesus. I guess I should have noticed somewhere along the way that Jesus chose to appear as a Palestinian Jew and every person who scratched out the divinely inspired pages of the Bible, both Old and New Testaments, was Jewish. A whole new world was uncovered for me while studying with Elijah and learning Jewish customs. But even though I learned from him that many of his people had trusted Jesus as their Messiah, and that excited me, I still hadn't found the right church.

Then one day it happened.

I was sitting in a big-building church service when God whispered to my heart, "Paul, *you* are my Church! And you are my house. I live in you and every other true believer!"

"What?" I said. "Did I hear you right?"

The original word for the New Testament church is *ekklesia*. The first time I tried to pronounce it, I started coughing. It has a unique sound and even when I say it today, I feel like I'm in one of the *Star Wars* movies pronouncing some spaceship name that I might be chasing. Like most words, church has different meanings as well. The New Testament biblical meaning of the word, however, is not a large brick and cement building where saints go to gather on Sunday mornings. Instead, it refers to people who are called out, those who make up the Body of Christ. The Bible tells us that individuals who have repented and believe in Jesus make up that Body of Christ. Period. And as far as bodies go, we each have parts of ourselves we are excited to show off, but we also have organs and certain valves that are private. But the bottom line is we need all of them. And the Church, that is, the Body of Christ, is the same. So I guess we need the guy like me who screws it all up for everyone else by doing something scandalous causing the God haters of the world to smile. They said, "See, there's no difference, he's just like me." I think if we meditated on this, or chewed on this concept while seeking the revelation of God, it would become active in us and we would have a little more unity. I'm not saying we need the sin. I'm just saying we need the person God loves and maybe it would be better to offer a helping hand rather than a pointed finger.

If I understand scripture correctly, one of the first warnings God gave Christians in the scriptures was not to separate over differences of opinion. It came as a result of the crazy lifestyled Corinthians who were dishonoring God, following and comparing different teachers and breaking off their relationships because of it. After two thousand or so years, I'm not sure that we're much different. I guess we build up walls.

Speaking of walls, I watched Mike Sweeney, at the time a hitter with Kansas City, pick up his bat and launch a bunch of baseballs over right-, left-, and centerfield walls during my time with the Royals. Mike was our team's best hitter and he hit a lot of home runs. Whenever there was a cool guest in the locker room, like a rock star or race-car driver, he always wanted to meet Mike. Since he was single at the time, a lot of cute teenage girls had Mrs. Sweeney T-shirts and when I teased him about that, he just laughed it off with a face that turned a little red. At first, I thought that Mike was too nice a person to get a lot of hits on the baseball field but I soon found out that he was like Roy Hobbs, one of the purest and most natural hitters I had ever seen. Swinging a bat seemed to be what he was born to do.

One of my favorite things to do with Mike was to walk with him from the parking lot into the clubhouse. It was a long journey that led down many flights of stairs and through a couple of tunnels that were a little grimy and always smelled, as janitors carted out trash from the previous day. I liked to make that journey on foot with Mike because he knew all the ushers, maintenance men, and sanitation engineers by their first names and when he asked them how they were doing he actually stopped and listened to their replies. He honestly cared about all of them. I had my favorites, but even then I didn't really know them and their stories like Mike did. I just nodded my head as I walked, thinking how I couldn't wait to get to the locker room to get the smell of trash and garbage out of my nose. While I detested that part of our route, Mike seemed to love it. So the journey was better with him and in a way that changed me.

I always asked Mike if he was going to run for governor when he was finished with baseball, knowing that he could win hands down, but I don't think that brownnosing or politicking held any interest for him. Mike just cared about people, all of them, not just famous musicians, race-car drivers, and big-salaried all-star players. He just loved and he loved everybody.

Each year Mike would organize a charity golf tournament to benefit the team chaplain for the Royals. Mike liked Jesus a great deal and often spoke about God's love for all people and how he felt it. Sometimes he would get choked up talking about God's love for us. He loved Jesus so much that even his teammates would make fun of him behind his back for being so overzealous.

One day I was signing autographs in the parking lot. I overheard a lady say to her friend, "Yeah, that Sweeney guy, he's a fake."

"How do you know?" her friend asked.

" 'Cause nobody's that nice!"

I just kept my head down and smiled as I signed another autograph wondering if I should be mean to the judgmental lady so she might take me as being authentic.

The only problem with Mike, at least in the eyes of mainstream evangelicals, rested in the fact that he was Catholic. His love for God confused people who were better at discerning correct doctrine, which included everyone who wasn't Catholic. So when those people had conversations with Mike it was only a matter of time before they tried to convert him and get him to stop praying to Mary, listening to the pope, and believing in purgatory.

A formal pastoral minister in another city wanted to meet with Mike one time so Sweeney agreed to go out to lunch with him. The man said he wanted to talk about Jesus and how his faith played out in the locker room but when Mike got there he found out that it was an ambush to get him corrected on the more right doctrine, which the pastor obviously had.

Mike responded by saying, "You might be right here and I might be right there and we can sit here all day and bicker about the finer points of our doctrine but in the end we are all a little off. No one but God has the perfect handle on every truth. I don't mind listening to you, if God has led you to challenge my beliefs, but I would rather talk about Jesus and the locker room, which is what I thought we came here to talk about in the first place."

Mike listened and considered the man's words, but I think he also realized that the man was primarily motivated to get him to see his point of view, while attacking Mike's beliefs. Although Mike personally believed in the exclusivity of Jesus and admitted that in other areas, his doctrine might be fallible, it wasn't good enough for the man.

Mike told me later, "I know the Catholic Church has been a little banged up over the years but so have a lot of other churches and denominations. I do a lot of work with youth groups and share the gospel with a lot of teenagers. They look up to me and tell me that it matters to them that even though I am famous and have a lot of money, I still love Jesus more than anything else. Paul, do you know how much that means to me? If I leave the Catholic Church, who will be there to share the gospel with those kids? I'm called to do that. Should I leave because someone else puts their specific calling on me? God hasn't shown me to do that."

I thought that was a beautiful response and I wondered if everyone who realizes that his denominational doctrine may be a little bit off should leave the place that God has allowed them to be when he called them. I was confused and thought of the verse that says, "A man should remain where he is when called." I guess that decision is one that each believer has to make for him or herself.

Over the years, I didn't necessarily leave the Catholic Church, I just began to do a cross-denominational ministry. Once when I thought I had settled on being nondenominational, I realized that the idea of not having a denomination had become sort of a denomination to me, causing me to look down on others who preferred something more specific. I guess I was sort of like the Pharisee who prayed hard to God and thanked him for not making him like the tax collector, which didn't go over too well with the Great Almighty.

So I began to notice Christ in many different individuals of various denominations despite their apparent or possible mistakes in minor doctrine, which again is often debated. I began to smile the most when I noticed people loving one another with the strength of Christ. I thought of another verse in that same letter to the Corinthians that says, "If I speak in the tongues of men and of angels, but have not love, I am only a resounding gong or a clanging cymbal. If I have the gift of prophecy and can fathom all mysteries and all knowledge, and if I have a faith that can move mountains, but have not love, I am nothing. If I give all I possess to the poor and surrender my body to the flames, but have not love, I gain nothing" (1 Corinthians 13:1–3 NIV).

The beauty of Mike Sweeney was simple—he loved people. Although he did believe that Jesus was the only way to the Father, many people seemed to miss his heart because there was a rosary draped over a brass coat hanger on the side of his locker. And that was sad to me.

Another teammate of mine in Kansas City during those same years was a man named David McCarty. We had also played baseball together years before on Team USA traveling to other countries while representing the United States. David had known me before I was a Christian so when I arrived at the stadium in Missouri he was suspicious of the new, hopefully Christlike me. David graduated from Stanford, was married to a pretty lawyer, and seemed too smart for Jesus. I got the feeling from him that Jesus was for people who needed a crutch. Therefore, he kind of became a master at teasing Christians, even though he always delivered his jokes in a humorous and most unthreatening way.

Standing six foot seven, he would stand up on a chair in our food room and say loudly in an Old English voice, "You're all going to burn, you godless heathens, burn! Do you hear me? Get that beer out of your hand! Get Beelzebub out of the locker room! Demons, be gone!"

It's not as funny on paper. I guess it's hard to communicate a funny accent with a pen or a computer keyboard.

David was my card partner on the plane flights and a good friend. Because it seemed so innocent and was so humorous, I never took offense at his mockery toward those of us who were professing Christians.

David called me one morning while we were on the road in Minnesota.

"Wake up, my friend," he told me. "I am going to take you to one of the coolest places you've ever been."

As we walked the streets of Minneapolis, I honestly had no idea where he could be taking me. I thought back to the years and places we had gone while in college playing summer baseball. I thought of the late nights after some of our games. I knew those places would be closed during the day so I relaxed. We walked for about twenty minutes until we stopped on Hennepin Avenue in front of a large building that looked like a massive church.

"There it is!" he said, announcing it to me with a sense of pride as if he had just pulled the vinyl cover off his prized antique Corvette.

"What?"

"That!"

"It's a big church?" I questioned with a tilted head and some confusion.

"Not just any church. It's the Basilica of St. Mary."

"A basilica?" I asked. "What is that?"

"Let me explain," David said. "A basilica is an ancient cathedral that has been given special ceremonial privileges by the pope. This just happens to be the oldest basilica in America, my friend. It was built in 1914. Wait till we walk inside. You're going to love it."

I laughed. David's line could have come out of a movie. He was the last person I would have ever taken to have the answer for my question or even bring me to a church for that matter. I looked around for a possible camera but I didn't see one. This was no prank. He was serious.

"Am I going in here to watch your godless heathen routine from atop one of the pews?" I asked.

"No! This is a place of holiness."

"Unlike the locker room," I asked.

"Exactly."

Once again, I laughed.

I was amazed at the architecture as we stepped inside. The ceiling was majestic with detailed carvings into stone and wood. It was as if every corner of the room was taken into consideration and deeply planned. The stained-glass windows were at least thirty feet tall and magnificent. They told biblical stories in their panes and I thought about all the teachings that they had soaked up through vibrations over the years. Words during the tough times our country went through, like the Great Depression and the two world wars. I walked across the marbled floor in awe and wondered if the designs could speak, what they would say and if they would testify about the risen Christ being the answer and very purpose to our lives.

I couldn't help but think that this is what I look like on the inside. *I am the real place where God resides*, I thought. *I too have been renewed and remodeled just like these stone bricks that were chiseled years ago. I have been pressure washed. I have windows into my soul that have been stained and reflect beauty when the Son shines through them.*

David and I had a great time that day but as we walked back to our hotel to get ready for the game, I thought about God's true church and what we have become and for some reason, I became a little sad. I hoped all of our differences could somehow be used by God.

I do wish there was some big-building church or group of people that had all the right answers about God. I wish there was a place where I agreed doctrinally with everything a group of people stood for but then again if that was the case maybe I would look to committees and voting boards to steer my thinking about God instead of just simply asking my Father, reading his word, and listening to him. After all, I have children and part of the fun of being a father is getting to interact with them myself and show them what I am all about firsthand. That's why regardless of whether or not I am in a small home group discussing Jesus or listening to a single man give a lesson before a large group of people or even walking into the baseball clubhouse for that matter, I am consciously aware that my spirit houses my Father, and

I rely on the Holy Spirit to teach me and grow me into a greater knowledge of him.

So I guess in retrospect, my wife was right when she laughed at me on that green canvassed couch in Cleveland and called me a postmodern fundamentalist. Maybe I really am, in the world's eyes, a big oxymoron after all. I say this because I now believe I have come into some kind of strange balance between all of the definitions and dynamics that make up the absolute Truth of Christ, my faith, my feelings, and my thinking with regard to the mysteries and house of God. And I have come to understand that above all these things, the love of God, which can spill out of my Spirit, is supreme. Not only does it bind the right answers together making them complete and perfect but also it covers a multitude of sins and mistakes that at times have seemed to cause confusion and separation in the true Body of Christ.

13

FAITH AND
THE HGH SCANDAL

MAHATMA GANDHI ONCE SAID, "If it weren't for Christians, I would become one." I suppose many people have had unpleasant experiences with born-again, Bible-thumping, Jesus-freaky Christians. Unfortunately, I am one of those to blame.

Even though I had Jesus in my life, and I didn't necessarily wound people with him, I just followed some sort of standard protocol of what I thought evangelical Christianity was all about. Sometimes I got a little off-track and hurt people with the formula of religion, similar to the subculture I talk about earlier in this book. For the most part, my time of behaving like a bounty hunter for Jesus was while playing minor league baseball with the Cleveland Indians in the early '90s shortly after I became a Christian.

During those couple of years, I used to walk out to batting practice carrying Xerox copies of chapters of Holy Scripture. I would say them aloud in the outfield. I committed entire epistles to memory. I mistakenly thought that God would like me better if

I behaved in such a manner and I envisioned a crowd of players walking over to be refreshed by the living water that was spewing out of my mouth because I had found a way to turn an hour of wasted time shagging fly balls into a holy teaching service.

Sad to say, I could not understand why only a few stray rabbits attended and my entire team stood at a distance on the other side of the field. I carried an extra-thick Bible on team plane flights, complete with tabs, in case I had any spur of the moment questions or was challenged to a debate by a fellow passenger. It was also heavy enough for me to slam it down like a gavel in case people didn't notice what I was reading.

Instead of the song "Fly Girl" or old-school rock and roll compositions coming out of my automobile speakers, I now could be heard blasting Christian praise music from about three blocks away. And when the car was stopped, I would occasionally run over to neighboring cars at stoplights and hand the drivers a conversion tract, especially if they were smoking. I hope I didn't cause any crashes during that time. But I probably did. I'm sure a few insulted people tried to run over me.

To make matters worse, I had fervent prayer time on a regular basis, sometimes kneeling like a Pharisee to impress not just the invisible God but all innocent bystanders as well. I even had a huge cross from my neck made from really large rusted nails, which left an indention in my chest after I pitched. Unfortunately, I had to tuck it inside my jersey when competing. The umpire said it was too much of a distraction to the hitter. I wore Christian T-shirts. Christian socks. Christian underwear. I could tell you a lot more but the trees in Tennessee don't produce enough paper and to be honest, I don't want to start vomiting.

Although I believe some of my intentions were actually good, my methods for stirring people to have faith in Christ were possibly a little off-track. I have a friend who is a Navy SEAL and he has an incredible intensity when sharing God, but I was never called to that type of witness. It wasn't me. I just followed the plan of what I thought was a good Christian soldier. But the good news for me and everyone else I encountered was that after my years as a Christian bounty hunter, I began to relax. I stopped begging people to come to Jesus. If they did not want Jesus to bring them to a Father who deeply loved them, I dusted off my shoes and walked away, hoping that I had planted a small seed that would someday germinate and grow. Sort of like Jesus who once asked the paralytic man, "Do you want to get well?" I realized that people had to *want* Jesus, and I couldn't force him on them. I learned that the Bible was right when it said that many would pick the larger and wider road that does not lead to him. And although self-destruction was sad to me, so was my begging.

After I began to calm down in my forced evangelistic efforts, I started to feel guilty about the way I had pressured people and damaged them in the name of religion. I think my eyes were opened to motives that I was previously unaware of and I noticed that I might have performed for God in my early years, hoping to ease my suffering over a past that wasn't too clean. I kept replaying the mental tapes in my head of the times where I tried to sell Jesus like he was some fabulous product on the Home Shopping Network that everyone needed. I had feelings of regret and disappointment and I wondered if I caused people to think like Gandhi and be turned off to Jesus.

In 2006, I chose to play baseball for the Cleveland Indians again. I loved Southern California and could have gone back to the Angels once more, or back to the Kansas City Royals to hang out in the Midwest with some of the best barbecuers and nicest people in the world. Close friends wanted to give me an IQ test when I turned down these comfortable places to play in a chilly town like Cleveland for less money. Not that I would be missing any meals while playing for any team in Major League Baseball, it just confused our close friends because our family didn't have any real ties to the city that was once referred to as the Mistake by the Lake.

So I just prayed and trusted that God could work through me at any of those places, not feeling any sort of strong leading from God toward any particular team or city. I think I picked Cleveland because my family would be closer to our home in Georgia than California, I respected our general manager Mark Shapiro, the team had an opportunity to win, and I would have a second chance at clearing my name from the first time around. You know, the guy who got people into spiritual chokeholds and earned the religious psycho label.

Our family found Cleveland to be anything but a mistake, experiencing passionate sports fans, meeting friendly neighbors, going to amusement parks, and soaking up the fantastic summer weather, which is the season of most importance to me. We even checked out the Rock and Roll Hall of Fame and managed to do some fly-fishing for championship steelhead.

I think God used Kym when we returned to Cleveland. Not only did she connect with a couple of wives, but she also sponsored the first ever Strong Marriages in Professional Sports Research Project, which was an investigation into the common strengths and weaknesses of athletes and their relationships off the field. This study not only looked at the common problems of a career-dominated marriage but documented the common traits of successful relationships, while at the same time dealt with those who managed to enjoy the game.

The locker room became another big-building church for me and I connected with a lot of my teammates, even the ones who didn't believe like me or regularly attend baseball chapel. After announcing Kym's research project to the team in spring training, I became sort of a poor man's Dr. Phil in the outfield, getting asked all sorts of questions about marriage. Only I didn't have as many answers as the famous talk show host. But after a while, I just relished the significant conversation that took place during batting practice—I mean, how many times can you go over the scouting report on Big Papi?

One time, while standing there with others, I thought back to my days in the minor leagues when I preached to the rabbits and quoted scripture to the sparrows. Almost instantly I became extremely appreciative of the simple fact that someone was standing next to me while I wore an Indians uniform. I hoped that I had represented Jesus a little better the second time around. And the possibility of doing so made me smile.

Another thing that made me smile while pitching for Cleveland was beating the Yankees and knocking them out of the playoffs in 2007. I didn't have any personal vendetta against the Bronx Bombers, I just hoped that becoming the winning pitcher would earn me a little more respect with Colby. After all, if I were any good, the Yankees would have traded for me. So after I won the clinching game in a zoolike atmosphere during playoff time in New York City, I gave an authenticated game ball to Colby, feeling proud of myself. He lost it before Christmas, however, which again left me feeling like Rodney Dangerfield, a man who gets no respect.

Sam Alipour, a reporter for *ESPN: The Magazine*, ran a featured article on me after that fateful game against the Yankees. Sam grew up in a Muslim household but said his heart and head lingered around this life with no real conviction toward any specific faith. I appreciated his honesty and attempt to write an article about something in an unbiased manner. We spent about two hours on the phone going over what I thought it meant to be a devout Christian and walk with God in Major League Baseball despite the temptations and difficulties in the locker room. Just as I enjoyed his sincere approach to getting an accurate story, I think he appreciated the fact that I didn't try to act like I was perfect or that all was well with me because I had received Jesus. I'm not sure why Sam wanted to write about my story in professional baseball but I really enjoyed his article. I was glad to hear his writing got a lot of positive and negative responses from both sides of the table. I guess whenever you talk about God—money, sex, or politics— there's going to be some arguments because almost every view ends up being controversial.

Speaking of controversy, days after our victory over the Yankees, I learned that a reporter in San Francisco wanted to get a comment from me before he released a story that named me as an alleged human growth hormone user during my time with the Royals and Braves shortly after the turn of the century. We were playing the Boston Red Sox at the time and if our team won another game, we would head to the World Series. For some reason, I had a strange peace about remaining silent. On our off day, I told the reporter through Bart Swain, our public relations coordinator, to go ahead and release his story. But it didn't happen. Instead, the story came out the morning of game seven, our last and final game with the Red Sox, running as the lead story for most major sports networks. I am not very good at assessing the deep and true motives of men, but this story seemed to have a political flavor to it before it ever turned through the silver printing wheels and that made me angry.

The breaking story implied that I had cheated for years by taking human growth hormone given to me by an antiaging clinic named Palm Beach Rejuvenation. Allegedly, one of the doctors at that clinic turned out to be a dentist whose license had expired. The article quoted statements from me earlier in my career where I encouraged kids to follow their dreams and to work hard to overcome any absence of talent by fanning into flame what God had given them. Now, by the tone of that article, it sounded as if I was a big fake and spiritual con artist who was using a performance-enhancing drug to carry me through my professional career; while not relying on God-given talent, or prayer, or hard work, or will, or bravery. The tone of the entire article bothered me deeply.

I sat on a red paisley sofa in a Boston hotel room for most of that morning and watched television as I ate at my breakfast. I listened to various reporters try to make sense of the situation without having any information from me. I kept trying to pray with words but the words just wouldn't come. Instead, I just sat there with God and watched, wondering if this article was going to do irreparable damage to people's view of my character.

I thought back to my time with the Indians long ago and the phase I went through when I felt I had embarrassed God and myself by introducing people to the counterfeit religion of legalism and Christian do's and don'ts, instead of Jesus Christ, the Person. After years of maturing and learning about grace, I felt like all that had been gained had been suddenly destroyed. I also wondered if I had damaged God's reputation and given someone like Gandhi another reason to reject the very Someone who loves him or her more than anyone else on this earth. Those thoughts made me sad and I could no longer eat.

I got up and took a look at myself in the mirror that morning, realizing that a wise man listens to correction, no matter how bad the timing and delivery or how publicly embarrassing the rebuke may be. I also knew that even though my conscience was clear concerning the way I had taken care of myself regarding therapeutic hormones, it still did not mean I was innocent. So, in order to check myself, I went over the details again in my mind. I had seen a licensed doctor in the Atlanta area due to weight loss, extreme insomnia, and chronic fatiguelike symptoms. After taking blood tests that revealed a deficiency, I was advised to start supplementing with growth hormone. I did so in normal amounts, which resulted in my ability to function like a normal person. After a short time, and for reasons unknown to me, that doctor transferred my records to Palm Beach Rejuvenation, a place where I did medical interviews over the phone and took regular blood tests to keep my levels regulated.

I had no way of knowing that a dentist was one of the staff members there. Nor did I know that some had suggested that the clinic had possibly violated some rules and regulations of standard medical practices; I just knew that I had a legitimate reason for taking the prescriptions that were written for me.

Besides knowing the legitimacy of the treatment that doctors in both Atlanta and Florida had prescribed, there have been two other doctors in other cities apart from Palm Beach who gave me different blood tests at various times and they all concluded that I had a need for taking the hormone. I also knew as I gazed at my reflection that morning that I had a tumor stuck on my pituitary gland, which could have been the culprit for some of my symptoms, and the FDA had approved the use of growth hormone to treat this type of deficiency. Something I had found out from an endocrinologist through working with the Cleveland Indians and the Major League Baseball drug-testing policy.

Not all doctors I had seen felt I should be supplementing with the hormone, but most did.

I hadn't tried to cheat or disrespect the game. I hadn't thrown the baseball any harder during the times I supplemented with growth hormone—in fact, I often got teased by my teammates for throwing the ball so slow   but I did enjoy sleeping more than four to five hours a night and I think that rest helped me recover *and throw bullpens* like a normal Major League Baseball pitcher. I also maintained my weight better and it helped my chronic fatigue. Frankly, I am a much better marriage partner and father when rested and both of these responsibilities are very important to me. In short, somewhere along the line I hit a bump in the road and when I supplemented with the growth hormone to maintain normal levels, I got my life back.

But like the other temptations I've mentioned in this book, I had a new one to deal with the first night I stuck that needle in a hormone-filled bottle. I wondered if I doubled my prescribed dose, whether or not I would throw harder and have a better and possibly longer career. After all, I had a prescription. At first, some strange silent voices ran across my brain and had conversations with me as I pulled back the syringe. I remember having thoughts that doing better on the field could mean more money for my family, my charities, and even supporting churches giving me the opportunity to become some sort of modern-day Robin Hood. Then I prayed and realized that God was in control of my life and he wouldn't want me making money through cheating the system. Unlike the night I siphoned gas from my neighbor leading to a damaged testicle, I didn't give in to the worldly temptation this time. I remembered the words of Wayne who said, "If you give people enough time to work things out in their heads, they can justify most any behavior, even murder." Voices of rationalization become very enticing when your dreams, physical satisfaction, and large amounts of money are on the line. I was thankful that with God as my strength, I was able to say no to those tempting voices.

As all these thoughts about my use of HGH were running through my head, I was told that numerous camera crews were waiting for me in the hotel lobby. My agent, Bo McKinnis, encouraged me to make a comment over the phone to Ken Rosenthal of FOX Sports. I was glad Bo asked me to talk to Ken because I trusted him as a reporter. He always seemed to quote players accurately and more important, he seemed to understand what athletes were trying to say even if their tongue fumbled the ball and they uttered something awkward. So I took a leap of faith that morning and prepared a small statement for Ken that explained I had a pituitary tumor and a documented need for supplementing the hormone. As soon as Major League Baseball required anyone supplementing with hormones to turn in paperwork, I complied with that rule, which gave me further peace about the situation and enabled me to tell Ken that I had notified the commissioner's office and my team. I also admitted to having shipments sent to locker rooms and team hotels under my name; something I felt meant one of two things, either I felt I had a legitimate prescription or my IQ consistently hung out well below the number 50. Ken wrote a very good article.

Faith and the HGH Scandal

Before I left for the field, Sam Alipour called me from *ESPN: The Magazine* and wanted to do a live interview, which absolutely scared me to death. I say this because anytime you talk or make a verbal mistake in front of a live audience it's very hard to take back. I was unsure of what I could say legally. I did know that my name constantly ran across the nation's sports radio talk shows and television broadcasts and watching and listening to those shows left me with a bad feeling in the pit of my stomach. I spoke with Sam that afternoon giving him details over the phone and letting him tell my story on ESPN through a live phone call. I watched Sam's interview on television and bit my cheek as he exposed my story of how I came to take the hormone and I listened to him explain my thoughts on Palm Beach Rejuvenation, a center that was now under investigation. Thankfully, he too did a good job of communicating my words but when it came time to close the interview, the ESPN reporter running the show asked him a heart-stopping question.

He said, "Sam, do you believe him?"

"What do you mean?" Sam asked.

"Well, we've heard the story but do you believe Paul Byrd. You know, personally?"

A couple of seconds passed as Sam sat there pondering the reporter's question. Sam had the opportunity to join many of the other reporters and commentators who were already filled with cynicism and judgment about me. But he didn't. Instead, he thought of his interaction with me and said rather calmly, "Yes, I do. I've talked to this guy and I believe him." And when he said that, I pumped my fist in the air!

I imagine it feels great to God when we put our faith in him and believe his story even when there are a few things that may not make sense to us. After all, faith would be nonexistent if there was no mystery left and we could solve God like a math problem. I've already tried worshipping things that can be figured out in this life and to be honest after a short while they become boring, which forces me to move on to something else. Therefore, I get excited at the fact that for the rest of my eternal days I will be able to grow in the grace and knowledge of God and continually taste his goodness while accepting the mysteriousness of his Person-hood.

Eventually, I left my hotel room and headed over to Fenway Park to play our last and final game against the Red Sox with the winner advancing to the World Series to play the Colorado Rock-ies. Opposing fans lightly harassed me as I got off the team bus and walked down to the locker room. It had rained a little that afternoon and reporters were everywhere as I walked through the historic steamy tunnel underneath the famous redbricked stadium where adoring fans once worshipped Ted Williams. I told the reporters as they approached me that I would make another state-ment before batting practice and I think they respected that effort from me, the night of such a crucial game.

I was supposed to go to the bullpen that night and be the first one called into the game if Jake Westbrook, our starting pitcher, got into trouble. I had beaten the Red Sox a few days prior and I couldn't wait to take the field, the same grass where I sat years before and watched Mark McGwire hit towering home runs off into the distance with amazing Grayson Byrd sitting on my lap. But Eric Wedge, our manager, told me that he wanted me to make a quick statement to the press and stay in our dugout during the game to avoid the possibility of unruly fans throwing things at me, calling me a cheater, and perhaps breaking out in unison chanting HGH, HGH, HGH.

Disappointment.

After addressing my teammates, Bart Swain said that I should say a sentence or two in front of reporters and walk away to batting practice. Having far more experience with the media than I, he wanted to protect me from saying something stupid or answering a question that could lead to a possible larger investigation. I grabbed the sheet of white typing paper that had my two generic declarative sentences and walked out of the locker room into the foggy tunnel again to a sea of eager reporters from around the world who were there to cover the playoffs. When I saw the mob of people I turned to Bart Swain and crumpled up the piece of paper, which made him cringe and turn his head away.

"What are you doing?" Bart asked, bringing his face back into focus.

"I'm sorry. I'm praying about this and I really feel like I have to explain a little bit more about the condition I was diagnosed as having and how I respect this game, the fans, and my faith."

"Oh my God!" he said. "Why are we deciding this now? Paul, I don't recommend this!"

Nevertheless, I adjusted my navy blue knee-high socks and proceeded to stand there for fifteen minutes, spilling my guts to everyone. I started by talking about the unpleasantness of the timing for my teammates and my family. Then I explained about my condition, being under a doctor's supervision, respecting the game, and caring about what kids and fans think of me when I walk into a stadium. And it was true, I didn't want the people who watch and make up our national pastime, which is so much about family and fatherhood, to believe that I had stayed afloat in the big leagues by cheating and taking a banned substance without reason. I also made mention of the fact that I had notified the Indians and Major League Baseball of my condition saying, "I am currently working with the Indians and MLB. They are aware of the fact that I have a pituitary gland issue."

I took about five questions and left for batting practice. Bart Swain was smiling at me and said, "Well that wasn't exactly what we had prepared but I think it went well." I agreed. During batting practice, I kept throwing baseballs to the Red Sox fans, kind of like peace offerings hoping to keep taunting words down to a minimum. For the most part, it worked.

Unfortunately, our team lost that decisive game to the Red Sox and we watched them celebrate on the field and climb on top of each other like mad men. Jake Westbrook had a good start, which left me sitting in the dugout experiencing the game from the wooden bench in the dugout. It was very tough for me to sit and watch us lose that game. Since I was a young boy, I'd desperately wanted to play in and win a World Series. But I had to remember the words of the Great DiMaggio who said I might help the Indians win a championship someday. Even though it wasn't exactly the one I had hoped to conquer, I did help my team win a divisional series by beating the Yankees a week before. It was just hard to find enjoyment out of anything at that particular moment, a time that turned out to be one of the hardest days of my life both on and off the field.

Tears started to fall in the locker room as grown men with hairy chests started to cry. And I was one of them. A reporter walked over to me during that time, looking angry while shoving a microphone in my face and saying, "Major League Baseball denies the report that you told them anything about taking HGH! Do you have any comment for them?" I wanted to punch him in the face but thankfully I didn't. It wasn't that I hated the reporter, I just didn't appreciate his timing and it certainly didn't look like he trusted any statement I had made, which in turn made me upset. I was exhausted.

Walking out into the tunnel one last time to go back to Cleveland, there were lines of Red Sox fans who stayed around to cheer and boo us as we left the building. Most of them were very classy and clapped for us as we walked the long trip back to the bus. I started the walk feeling a little embarrassed after learning that Major League Baseball had denied my claim that I informed them of my HGH usage. Dressed in a suit, I wondered if I looked like a fraud to people or someone who played the Jesus card with ulterior motives and I remembered the words of my father Larry the Legend when he said the two most crooked professions he ran across were law enforcement and religious organizations.

I got mixed reviews leaving Fenway Park; I would walk past people who gently clapped and then silence. In one instance there were headshakes of disapproval followed by a man who yelled out, "Cheater!" Then someone in the back yelled, "Stay strong, brother! Keep the faith!"

I walked a few more yards to a group of college students who were waiting for me. Like a well-trained college fraternity, they started chanting, "HGH! HGH! HGH!" Again, I had this awful feeling in the pit of my stomach and I felt like a big fake.

But before long a girl who was probably in her early twenties, emerged from the crowd and made her way toward me saying as loud she could, "I believe you, Paul Byrd!" It was music to my soul and I should have stopped to hug her but I didn't. Instead, I just smirked and nodded my head to her as I kept walking fearing a public emotional collapse if I paused to thank the young lady. I was deeply moved when she made her statement of belief in me, when it looked to so many that I was a liar. In some small way, it was another statement of faith.

I thought back to Jesus when he walked among the people while carrying a heavy wooden cross among the divided words that were screamed out for and against him. His face and back dripping blood as he walked out to a hill name Golgotha, his place of known execution. I thought about the fact that he willingly chose to make himself a man of no reputation and the extreme pressure he must have felt amid the cries. But mostly, I thought about the reason he endured and labored: because he loved so many people, including me.

Here I was about to have a breakdown, and I was just trying to get to an air-conditioned yellow tour bus to go to the airport so I could get home and hide out until the smoke cleared. I thought about how much I loved myself and how much I wanted to defend myself at every turn. And how much I cared about letting everyone know I was right. Suddenly, I felt selfish.

In the end, I am not sure why parts of my story did not check out with Major League Baseball. I am currently under investigation by their lawyers and will have to wait and see if I am suspended. I don't think their legal team is out to unfairly get the players; they just want to get the truth and clean up the image of baseball so that there is a great deal of integrity left in the game. Our national pastime has been very reliable over the years, answering the call to world wars, and stimulating the public out of fear in times of great disasters like the bombing of the Twin Towers, an earthquake and aftershocks in San Francisco, and the bridge collapse in Minnesota. And I, for one, believe it needs to stay that way.

Regardless of the upcoming verdict that Major League Baseball will hand out concerning me, I am still guilty in this life. Maybe not the way I handled my hormone usage, but with other things and I am not fully trustworthy either. I have mentioned so many of my failures and weaknesses throughout this book, times where my flesh has picked a counterfeit life source and chosen someone or something over God.

I hope that my transparency will help someone else who might struggle with their own versions of wrestling with Eddie Perez, or wondering why bad things happen to them. Or when men struggle against pornography or in relating to their own Larry the Legend. I hope some of my weird-sounding stories like the time I asked God to be my pitching coach will encourage others to involve the Creator in everything they do.

One of the most incredible gifts of freedom for me has come through the past few months in dealing with the media, lawyers, trainers, doctors, an agent, and myself. It has been the undeniable fact that God is the only One who is truly faithful and trustworthy. I think the central verse in the Bible says it is so much better for us to put our faith in God than in man and I have found such a freedom in experiencing this verse to once again come alive and be true. Similar to the night I pitched against Randy Johnson, I find myself right back at the beginning of my book even though I am at the end, trusting in God to be my deliverer. I have learned through it all that true liberty comes in experiencing a real relationship with God. That relationship is made possible through the person of Jesus. And connecting to him has made me a Free Byrd.

ACKNOWLEDGMENTS

First off, even though I have a Mac, I would like to thank whoever developed Microsoft Word. Your including a thesaurus under the "tools" tab saved a verbally challenged athlete like me many hours and helped me include interesting adjectives for my audience. I also would like to thank my high school literature teachers, especially Mike Johnson, for being so enthusiastic and making poems and short stories come alive for me. Thanks as well to the sometimes hard-to-hear writing critiques from fellow students and professors at LSU. Years later, I can honestly say your sometimes stinging criticisms have made me a better writer.

A special thank-you to my two boys, Grayson and Colby, for stirring a love inside me that caused me to begin writing again. Thank you to Ben Ortlip, a talented writer near my home in Alpharetta, Georgia, for encouraging me and insisting that I seek a publisher. Thanks to David Sanford, my literary agent, for taking me on not just as a client but also as a new friend. You and your team have been helpful at every turn. Thanks for making my book-publishing dream come true.

Thank you to James Keating, a genius of the English language and former editor of *BusinessWeek*, for sitting me down in

ACKNOWLEDGMENTS

Chicago and telling me that my stories engaged you from a place deep within. Thank you to Denny Boultinghouse and Susan Wilson at Simon & Schuster for working around the clock to edit this manuscript and pull everything together. Both of you have helped me to appreciate that different perspectives are a good thing!

Thank you to my friend Robert Orr, who spent countless hours on the computer critiquing my rough drafts. You spent more time than anyone thinking and praying about my book. I so appreciate all you did. You deliver.

Finally, thank you to my amazing wife, Kym, for spending many years of your life with me and forcing me to talk and express myself when I have wanted to give a simple response about my day, like, "It went well." I could not have written a book without you.

NOTES

CHAPTER 1:

BEATING RANDY JOHNSON AND THE TROUBLE WITH DAVID

1. Peter Kreeft (ed.) and Blaise Pascal, *Christianity for Modern Pagans: Pascal's Pensées* (London: Penguin Classics, 1966), 232.

CHAPTER 3:

THE GREAT DIMAGGIO AND THE CHRISTIAN SUBCULTURE

1. Ernest Hemingway, *The Old Man and the Sea* (New York: Simon & Schuster, 1995 ed.), 17.

CHAPTER 4:

TRYING TO GET LIFE AND ACCEPTANCE FROM
THE PAGES OF *PLAYBOY* MAGAZINE

1. Shelley Lubben, "The Truth Behind the Fantasy of Porn," www.shelleylubben.com/articles (accessed December 12, 2007).

CHAPTER 5:

AMAZING GRAYSON!

1. Brennan Manning, *The Ragamuffin Gospel: Good News for the Bedraggled, Beat-Up, and Burnt Out* (Colorado Springs: NavPress, 2002), 25.

2. Dietrich Bonhoeffer, *The Cost of Discipleship* (New York: Touchstone, 1959), 44–45.

NOTES

CHAPTER 8:

THE MAGNIFICENT PERFORMANCE OF COLBY BYRD

1. The Official Web Site of Vince Lombardi, "Number-One Speech," www.vincelombardi.com/about/speech.htm.

CHAPTER 9:

JACOB WRESTLED GOD; I WRESTLED EDDIE PEREZ

1. Gordon Dalbey, *Healing the Masculine Soul: God's Restoration of Men to Real Manhood* (Nashville, Tenn.: W Publishing Group, 2003), 33.

2. You can read the full story in Genesis 32.

CHAPTER 10:

WHEN BAD THINGS HAPPEN TO GOOD BASEBALL PLAYERS

1. Harold S. Kushner, *When Bad Things Happen to Good People* (New York: HarperCollins, 1981), 6.

MORE ONLINE

If you enjoyed this book, visit www.freebyrdbook.com, where you can:

- download a discussion/application guide
- see more photos of Paul Byrd in action
- read Paul's current blog postings
- watch clips from his latest TV interviews
- check out his upcoming schedule
- send an e-mail to Paul
- and more!